CW01497595

G R A ....P L E

LOOK

AT SIGNATURE

AND
Shock & Impress Someone By Finding Their Outer Personality With Graphology Signature Analysis. Discover Your Outer Self

ANALYZE

First Name
Confident
Open Mind
Suicidal?
...?

PUBLIC PERSONALITY

PASSIONATELY WRITTEN BY

AKHILESH BHAGWAT

Copyright ©2022 by Akhilesh Bhagwat

All rights reserved. No part of this book may be reproduced, distributed, or transmitted in any form or by any means, including photocopying, recording, or other electronic or mechanical methods, without the prior written permission of the author, except in the case of brief quotations embodied in critical reviews and certain other noncommercial uses permitted by copyright law

KDP ISBN 9798801876269

This Book Is Dedicated To My Brave Dad, Beautiful Mom and Sweet Small Sister Anuja!

Contents

1] BASICS

Getting Basics Right!

2] NAMES

Independent or Family Oriented

3] SPACING

How Much Close Are You With Your Family?

4] Underlines

How many underlines do you have?
0...1...2...3...?

5] LEGIBLE/ILLEGIBLE

Is your name easily readable?

6] DOTS

How many dots do you have? Where are those dots placed?

7] SIZE

Well In Signature SIZE Does Matter!

8] DIRECTION

**Which direction do you follow?
Upwards or Downwards or Straight?**

9] SLANTS

**Well do you take Emotional Decisions
or Logical Decisions?**

10] PLACEMENTS

**Do you sign on left side or on right side
or in middle?**

11] PRESSURE

HIgh Energy or low energy!

12] SPEED

Nervous or confident?

13] NEGATIVE TRAITS

Avoid these signatures at all cost!

14] EXTRA-1: LETTER TRAITS

Letter Types in Signatures & Their Meaning

15] EXTRA-2: ADVANCE CONCEPTS
Different Conditions

16] ANALYSIS

Time For Demo

17] GRAPHOTHERAPHY

Making Changes In Signature

18] SOMETHING MORE!

Where To Go From Here?

1] LOOK AND ANALYZE

1

Introduction

My Story

I was a very shy person due to which I was not able to communicate with new people, in order to improve this I started reading body language books, changed my body language yet it didn't helped much due to which I again got frustrated, felt sad for myself. As this was happening during my college days I was writing lot of stuff, assignment, journals so one day I just got curious as why I write like this? Why my friend is having different handwriting & I have different one? Is there any reason behind it just like body language? So I just googled "why we have different handwriting" & after reading various blogs I got a blog on Graphology.

Curiosity got me & I kept reading one blog to another to learn more and more about Graphology. I read a blog on "how to find extrovert from handwriting, sign" it was about large

2] LOOK AND ANALYZE

size handwriting, sign. I thought what if I change my handwriting, sign size?

With practice I started writing with large size & I don't remember exactly yet after a month or two I was just able to talk with strangers which before was not easy.

Next up was confidence so I read another blog which was about letter t, adding high t bar helped me in increasing my confidence & my self-image after that I added many more changes & my life started improving.

Now since I wanted to learn more yet there was no educational page on Graphology on insta I decided to start one, also I wanted to give back this knowledge which helped me improve. At the start I just posted pictures about Graphology and then it went to videos, blogs, courses & now book.

So Graphology helped me in becoming a public speaker from a shy person. It can help you as well. We have often told to change our thoughts to change personality and it's not that easy yet there is one way to improve your personality and change your thoughts, that way is Graphology

3] LOOK AND ANALYZE

Handwriting analysis and signature analysis are the 2 units of Graphology and here we are going to study about signature analysis.

If you are getting started in Graphology then signature analysis is the key as you will learn complete signature analysis more faster as core concepts here are less. After signature analysis you can move to handwriting

After reading this book I believe the way you used look at signature will significantly change.

You will be able to shock, impress anyone by finding their personality with just signature. "I am impressed", "You are a magician", "How can you get to know so much about me?", "Whatever you said is so trueee!", I get feedbacks like this whenever I do the analysis and now you will get same after you do analysis. The book has been written in a such a way that you can start doing analysis from first page. Just look at sample and then find the trait related to that sample. For eg- If you observe first name in sample then find first name trait in the book

4] LOOK AND ANALYZE

BEFORE STARTING OUR JOURNEY

- Take a blank paper
- Now take a blue ball pen, black will also work (No Gel or ink or sketch pen or pencil)
- Sign your own signature, take sign sample of your family members, friends.
- You can also download your favorite celebrity, mentor signature samples from the internet as well!
- Get as many sign samples as you can!
- Tip: Check Signature samples in between as you learn new concepts (Analyze Yourself First)
- This will help you learn Graphology signature analysis in a more practical way as you are applying knowledge as soon as you learn it.

Basics

GETTING BASICS RIGHT!

7] LOOK AND ANALYZE

GRAPHOLOGY

How Does It Work?

YOU

We Daily think lot of thoughts, feel lot of emotions. Now we cannot share every feeling, emotions with others

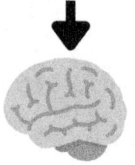

YOUR BRAIN

And if not shared such feelings can lead to depression, overthinking. So a outlet is needed to remove those emotions

YOUR HANDWRITING, SIGN

Our Brain Finds that outlet through our handwriting and signature. Every feeling, emotions is then transported from brain to your handwriting, signature

8] LOOK AND ANALYZE

1] Graphology

- In Simple Words, Graphology is a science of finding someone's whole personality with handwriting, sign.
- Some Practical Examples Which Proves Graphology Works:
- At the start of exam your mind is clear henceforth handwriting is clear whereas during last 10 minutes your mind is running faster henceforth handwriting is dirty or messy!
- We have always being told to do journaling or write our emotions down. And whenever we write down our emotions we automatically feel calm. You know why? Because your brain transfers all those emotions into handwriting, signature
- Observe yourself whenever you feel happy you look up while being sad you look down. Same concept is here
- Most poet, artists handwriting, sign is always tilted in right direction. In graphology it shows creativity
- Most of the introverts always have small handwriting, extroverts have large size. You can check your friend's handwriting

9] LOOK AND ANALYZE

COMPARISON BETWEEN SIGN, HANDWRITING ANALYSIS

Handwriting Analysis

1. Handwriting is all about your private personality
2. It reveals writer's real personality
3. Writer cannot hide his/her true self here as handwriting reveals everything.
4. Handwriting analysis have more than 5000+ traits as each letter have more sub categories
5. Handwriting analysis is just a way of finding personality by just looking at handwriting elements like letters
6. It takes more time to learn Handwriting Analysis as concepts are more
7. It is hard to find someone's handwriting sample as we often sign more be it in attendance sheet, casual signs, etc.

10] LOOK AND ANALYZE

COMPARISON BETWEEN SIGN, HANDWRITING ANALYSIS

Signature Analysis

1. Signature is all about your public personality
2. It tells how writer want others to see him as
3. Sometimes a writer show something different in front of others and in reality they are different
4. Signature analysis have 100+ core concepts
5. Signature analysis is the science of finding someone's personality by looking at signature elements like underlines, dots
6. If you are getting started in graphology then you can first start with sign analysis as you will master it quickly as compared to handwriting
7. You will often find someone's sign more

11] LOOK AND ANALYZE

WHAT DOES SIGN REVEAL ABOUT SOMEONE?

Akhilesh

@ABhagwat

Walt Disney

large size   small size
↓   ↓
Akhilesh Bhagwat

Benny Dab

Henry   X unt
         formed

12] LOOK AND ANALYZE

WHAT YOUR SIGN SAYS?

- Sign represent your public self-image.
- It shows how you behave in public & act around people.
- It's about what you want others to think about you
- With time the way of signing up may change based on job such as doctors, leaders, etc.
- By just sign you cannot get complete picture of writer.
- Both handwriting, sign are needed so learning both is important
- Signature can help you know if writer is faking their personality or is true person
- You can get to know how much social confidence a writer is having, who gets first priority family or self, how much open is the writer and will they open up if you try to talk, writer likes being in front or likes working behind the scenes. Many amazing and interesting things can be found!

13] LOOK AND ANALYZE

___

WHY SIGN ONLY REVEALS PUBLIC PERSONA?

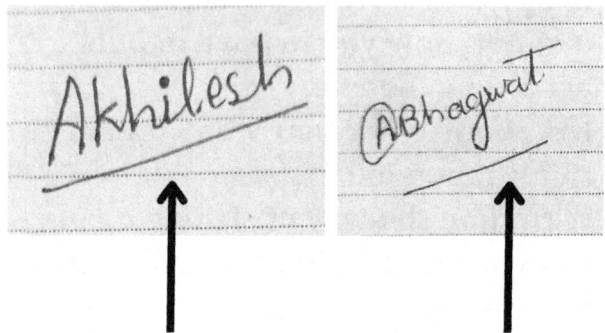

Only Names Are Present, There's No Expression of emotions, feelings

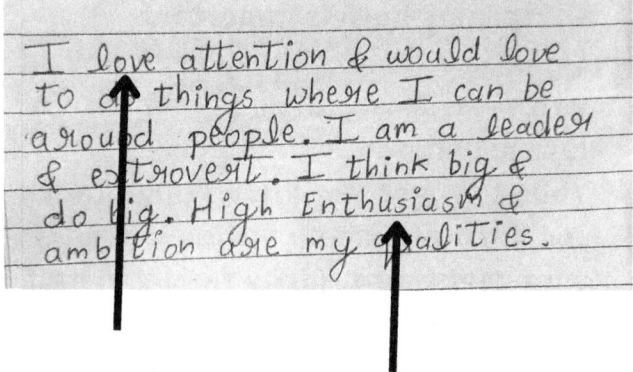

You can find "Love", "Enthusiasm" like words which are emotions & expression

14] LOOK AND ANALYZE

WHY NOT PRIVATE PERSONA?

- In handwriting you write sentences, words which are about different topics yet in sign you only write names.
- Those words and sentences communicate your feelings for others directly like word "happy", "sad", "love" etc. help you know what you are really feeling yet in sign just names cannot tell what are you feeling so your real private feelings are not shown in sign.
- And your name reveals only about you!
- Another person cannot know what you feel about them or about a particular thing.
- Since signature cannot reveal true feelings directly via words it only reveals public persona
- As to know real feelings you need to know real emotions, feelings

Name

WHO GETS FIRST PRIORITY?

17] LOOK AND ANALYZE

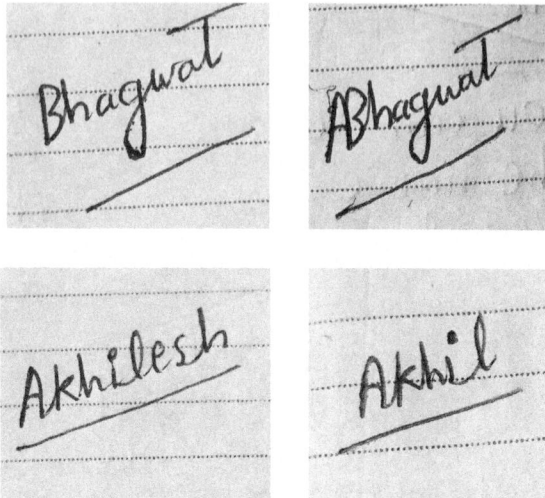

3

What Name Do You Write?

With name you can know if a writer is an

- Independent person
- Someone who doesn't take himself/herself seriously
- Is someone who make sacrifices for others
- More attached towards family.
- A balanced individual
- In short, it tells about ego, priorities of the writer

19] LOOK AND ANALYZE

ONLY FIRST NAME

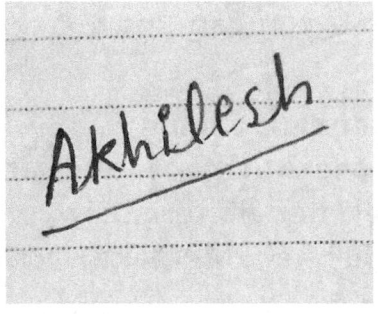

Brad

Anuja

Salman

Amitabh

20] LOOK AND ANALYZE

HOW TO FIND?

- Ask the writer what name they have written in their signature
- Sometimes we think it's first name yet it's not. For eg- Rohit could be first name as well as last name.
- So always ask the writer!

WHAT IT INDICATES?

- Only first name means only self. Writer here gives herself/himself the first priority.
- Writer here wants to show others that he/she is independent, have pride about self.
- They have strong sense of self yet do not stick too closely with family

WHO SIGN LIKE THIS?

Shahrukh Khan, Amir Khan

21] LOOK AND ANALYZE

___

ONLY LAST NAME

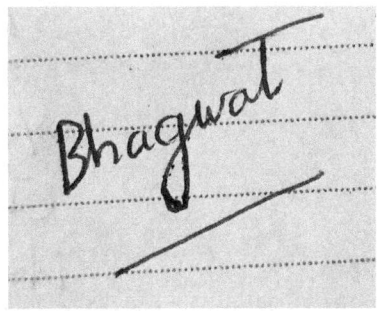

Tendulkar

Picasso

22] LOOK AND ANALYZE

HOW TO FIND?

- Just like first name here too ask the writer what name they have written in their signature
- Sometimes we think it's first name yet it's not. For eg- Rohit could be first name as well as last name.

WHAT IT INDICATES?

- Last name means only family as here writer has written his/her last name instead of first or both names which shows what is more important for writer
- Here writer is attached with family, gives them first priority in most situations
- These people are loyal yet they may feel uncomfortable outside family protection

WHO SIGN LIKE THIS?

Sachin Tendulkar, Pablo Picasso

23] LOOK AND ANALYZE

FIRST NAME INITIAL & FULL LAST NAME

Full Last Name

Instead of "Akhilesh" it's "A" here

B. R. Ambedkar

A. Einstein

Along with first name,
father name's initial is also present

24] LOOK AND ANALYZE

HOW TO FIND?

- Here signature do not have full first name instead only first letter is there.
- In some samples Father's or Mother's or Husband's initial is also present in between

WHAT IT INDICATES?

- These people make sacrifices for others and give family, others more priority as you can observe only one letter of first name is there so less about self & more about family
- Hardworking individual having more attachment towards mother or father or anyone who's name initial is also present
- Responsible people in nature, many parents have this trait

WHO SIGN LIKE THIS?

B. R. Ambedkar, Albert Einstein

NICK NAME

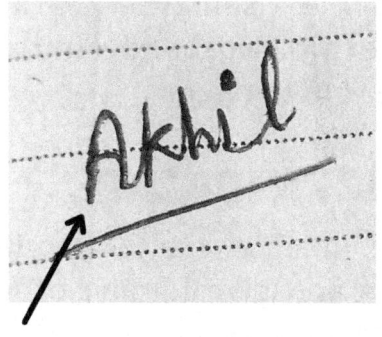

Full name is not written instead of "Akhilesh" it's "Akhil"

Apple Co-founder Steve Wozniak writes "Woz" instead of Wozniak

HOW TO FIND?

- Ask the writer if it's their first name or last name or nick name

WHAT IT INDICATES?

- Just like first name these people are also independent in nature.
- They are stubborn as well so they keep holding on to their opinions
- First name and nick name sign have many same qualities, the only main difference here is writers here don't take themselves that much seriously

WHO SIGN LIKE THIS?

Apple Co-founder Steve Wozniak

27] LOOK AND ANALYZE

FULL NAME

Akhilesh Bhagwat

Full First Name + Full Last Name

Akhilesh A Bhagwat

Full First Name + Initial of parent or husband/wife + Full Last Name

28] LOOK AND ANALYZE

HOW TO FIND?

- Writer's full first name as well as last name is present.
- Here too you will often find initial in between.

WHAT IT INDICATES?

- If only first name shows self and only last name shows family then what would combination of both say?
- It says writer give equal priority to both self as well as family, others
- These people have balanced approach towards life, self
- They focus on personal as well as professional goals
- One of ideal sign, many people have this type of signature!

WHO SIGN LIKE THIS?

Amitabh Bachchan, Lata Mangeshkar, Jeff Bezos, Charlie Chaplin, Bill Gates, Steve Jobs

Spacing

FIND HOW MUCH
CLOSE A PERSON IS
WITH THEIR FAMILY

31] LOOK AND ANALYZE

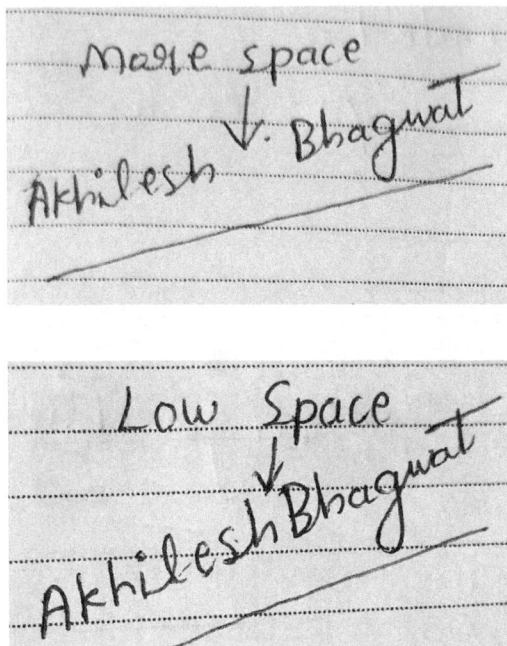

4

Spacing between names

Spacing is often overlooked yet it is also an important trait as you can know
- How much close a writer is between himself & his father, mother, husband, wife, family
- Spacing have 2 main types low, high, and each tells different things about the writer
- You can only find this trait if writer have both first name & last name

---

MORE SPACING

More Space

Akhilesh V. Bhagwat

More Spacing where initial is also present

Less Spacing between First Name & Initial and more Spacing between Last name & First name

34] LOOK AND ANALYZE

HOW TO FIND?

- Observe distance between first name & last name.
- Sometimes if an initial is present then observe spacing between first name, initial & then first name, last name

WHAT IT INDICATES?

- Here writer keeps more distance between himself, family.
- They don't feel more closeness with family
- Rule of thumb is more the spacing more the isolated, reserved the writer is
- During early days, married women tend to have more spacing between last name yet it decreases with time once they feel comfortable

WHO SIGN LIKE THIS?

Young Married Women

LESS SPACING

Low Space

↓

Akhilesh Bhagwat

Akhilesh A Bhagwat

Less Spacing between all names

36] LOOK AND ANALYZE

HOW TO FIND?

- Same just observe the distance if it's too low then writer fall under this category

WHAT IT INDICATES?

- Less the distance more the writer feel closeness with the family.
- Family oriented people
- Remember No distance indicates attachment. So keep it balanced
- Same is for initials be it of father, mother, wife, husband or anyone
- Less the distance between first name and initial more the closeness writer feels with that individual.
- For eg- First Name "Akhilesh" and "A" (Father's Initial) are close then it shows writer feel closeness with his father

WHO SIGN LIKE THIS?

Family oriented individual

Underlines

HOW MANY UNDERLINES DO YOU HAVE? 0...1...2...3...?

UNDERLINES

5

All About Underlines

Underlines are like the base of your public image. It can help you know lot about a person's
- Ego, self awareness.
- Lot more things such as if they follow any set of rule to live life or just keep going with flow.
- Mainly you will find 3 types of common underline in most signatures yet we will study 5 of them.
- The line above the name is known as Overscore

41] LOOK AND ANALYZE

SINGLE UNDERLINE

Only 1 Underline is present

42] LOOK AND ANALYZE

HOW TO FIND?

- If any writer have 1 line below their signature then they fall under this category....very simple!

WHAT IT INDICATES?

- Writers here are confident about themselves, about who they are
- These people have healthy ego and life values
- Also these people have some rules or standards about life which they tend to follow
- One of the ideal trait to have
- Many successful people have this trait
- These writers also have leadership qualities and good amount of self-belief

WHO SIGN LIKE THIS?

Amitabh Bachchan, Shahrukh Khan

43] LOOK AND ANALYZE

DOUBLE UNDERLINE

Only 2 Underline is present

44] LOOK AND ANALYZE

HOW TO FIND?

- If any writer have 2 line below their signature then they fall under this category yet remember it must be only 2 underline not 3 or more than that!

WHAT IT INDICATES?

- There are 2 types of leaders one who people naturally follow and other who force others to follow them
- These people fall in second category as they tend to force their opinions, values on others as they want to be seen as an important person.
- They also often feel incomplete or imperfect.
- And become aggressive or feel low if their opinions are not accepted by others. Sign of low esteem.

WHO SIGN LIKE THIS?

My friend henry. Check your friend's sign to see who sign like this!

45] LOOK AND ANALYZE

MORE THAN 2 UNDERLINE

Signature

More Than 2 Underline is present

Akhil

Henry Smith

4 UNDERLINES

46] LOOK AND ANALYZE

HOW TO FIND?

- If any writer have more than 2 line below their signature then they fall under this category. Now underline could be 3 or 4 or 5 or even 8 and all fall under this same category

WHAT IT INDICATES?

- 1 underline tells you have good principles, ego so if you try to overdo the underline it then it indicates opposite!
- These writers are confused about self, about who they are.
- Unable to make firm decisions
- Not the ideal trait to have
- You will rarely find this trait

WHO SIGN LIKE THIS?

Some very unique people

47] LOOK AND ANALYZE

OVERSCORE

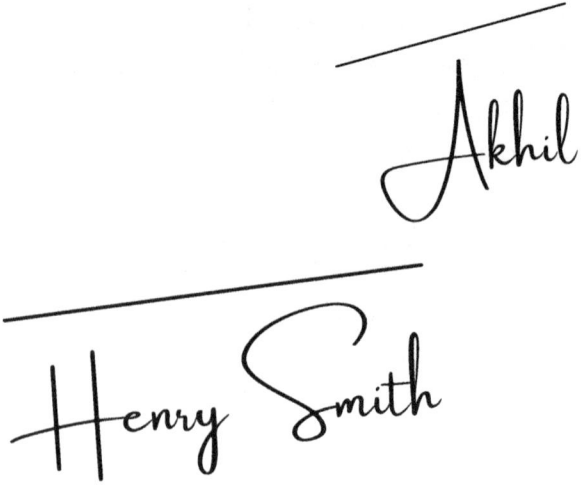

Line is above the name

48] LOOK AND ANALYZE

HOW TO FIND?

- Writer who have 1 underline above the name fall under this category

WHAT IT INDICATES?

- So firstly overscoring signifies selfishness, self-protectiveness. It's like writer is trying to protect by adding a roof (Underline) above their head
- Keeps Changing in character which do not allow writer to show himself/herself clearly and getting across
- Their ideas, thinking pattern also keeps changing leading to contradiction
- Again this sign is also a Rare Type

WHO SIGN LIKE THIS?

Some very rare people

ZIG-ZAG UNDERLINE

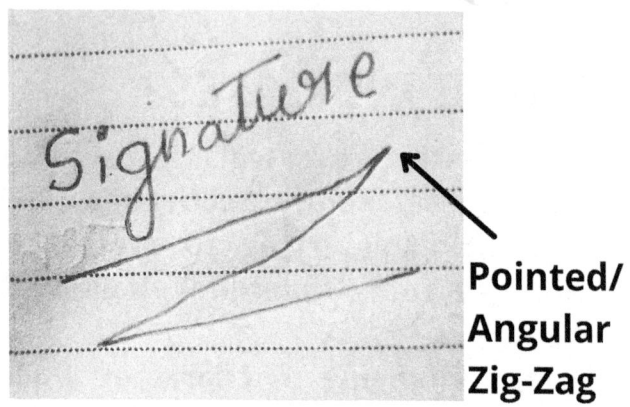

Pointed/
Angular
Zig-Zag

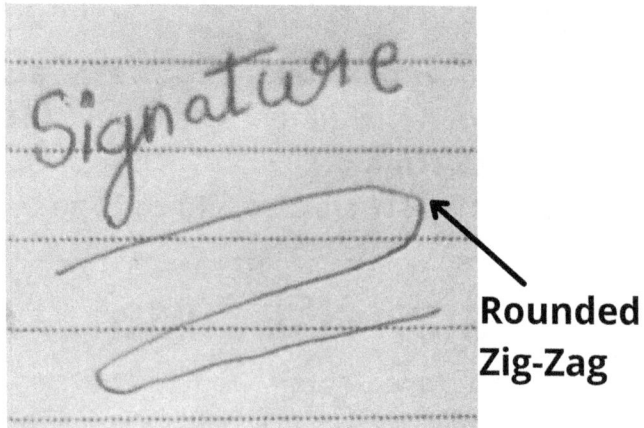

Rounded
Zig-Zag

50] LOOK AND ANALYZE

HOW TO FIND?

- Underline is formed in "Z" shape
- It could be pointed or rounded

WHAT IT INDICATES?

- Zig-Zag underlines are of two types, one is pointed another is rounded
- Writer having pointed curve are aggressive in nature, do not just commit easily
- Writer having normal curve are more calmer in nature and can commit more quickly
- In both cases line goes back and again go forward it means writer says something now yet in future may do opposite.
- They don't keep their words

WHO SIGN LIKE THIS?

Some very rare people

51] LOOK AND ANALYZE

BROKEN UNDERLINE

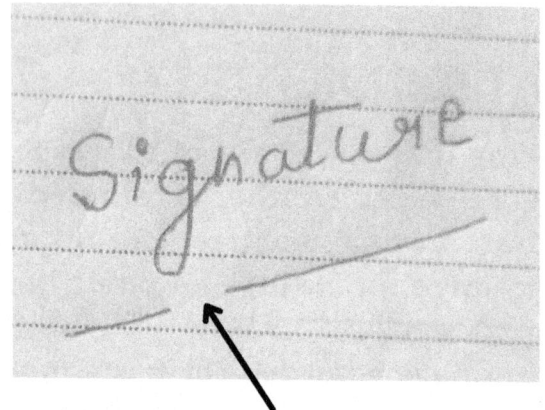

Underline is broken in between

Bhagwat

Pushpa

52] LOOK AND ANALYZE

HOW TO FIND?

- Here underline is broken in between
- It could be below whole sign or in between letters

WHAT IT INDICATES?

- Underline is like the base of your signature and a broken base is not good right?
- Here writer do not have healthy ego.
- They also have partial confidence.
- Due to this they are not fully sure about themselves, decision they are taking.
- They keep thinking, "Should I do this" or "Should I not"
- If you sign like this then join the underline & don't break it

WHO SIGN LIKE THIS?

Again it's a rare type sign

53] LOOK AND ANALYZE

___

NO UNDERLINE

Signature

No Underline

Ratan Tata

Mukesh Ambani

Arnold Schwarzenegger

54] LOOK AND ANALYZE

HOW TO FIND?

- Very Simple...If you see a signature which doesn't have any underline below then that writer fall in this category

WHAT IT INDICATES?

- Underline indicates that a person want their presence felt while no underline indicates opposite
- Writers here don't feel the need to prove themselves, impress others.
- They are ok with not being recognized, given attention
- You can find many people who had done very great work yet don't like showing off in front of media instead they keep doing their work. For eg- Ratan Tata Sir

WHO SIGN LIKE THIS?

Ratan Tata, Mukesh Ambani, Arnold Schwarzenegger

Legibility

IS YOUR NAME EASILY
READABLE?

57] LOOK AND ANALYZE

You cannot clearly read the name (all letters).

You can read the name clearly

6

Legible/Illegible Signatures

Now sometimes you will find signatures where names are not readable. While some people write their name so clearly that it's clearly readable even from a distance. Both people have different personality traits. Here you can find:

- If she/he is an open person who interact with others
- Or a private person who will not open up unless they know you.
- There's another category in between where people are open about some parts of life and reserved about rest
- Legible (Readable), semi-legible, illegible (Not readable) signature can help you know the writer's interaction with others

---

LEGIBLE SIGNATURE

Akhilesh

You can read
the name
clearly

Ratan Tata

Jeff Bezos

Bill Gates

HOW TO FIND?

- If you can read writer's name or letters in the sign clearly without putting much effort & even from a small distance then writer fall under this category

WHAT IT INDICATES?

- Open minded individuals who have nothing to hide.
- Straightforward people
- They adapt to new things quickly & tend to know themselves the reason they are confident about who they are
- Can be understood by others, have clarity of thoughts
- Many top entrepreneurs have legible sign as to innovate, create new things you need to be an open-minded person

WHO SIGN LIKE THIS?

Ratan Tata, Steve Jobs, Bill Gates, Jeff Bezos, Walt Disney

61] LOOK AND ANALYZE

ILLEGIBLE SIGNATURE

illegible

Semi-Legible

You cannot clearly read the name (all letters)

Google "Keanu Reeves Sign", "Tom Hardy Sign" to see an illegible sign as you cannot fully read their name

Google "Elon Musk Sign" or "Barack Obama Sign" to see a semi-legible sign as you can only read E, M and O, B in their name

62] LOOK AND ANALYZE

HOW TO FIND?

- Here you need to put effort to understand what name is written, sometimes it's not even readable so you need to ask writer which letters are present in sign

WHAT IT INDICATES?

- These are private, reserved type people who don't just open up to everyone
- Just like their name is hard to read these people are also hard to understand, read. You need to gain their trust first
- Many fast thinkers also tend to have this type like doctors
- Semi-legible signature tells that person is anxious, impatient
- Tom Hardy is known for being most private celebrity and you can find this in his signature as it's illegible

WHO SIGN LIKE THIS?

Tom Hardy, Keanu Reeves, Elon Musk

DOTS

HOW MANY DOTS DO YOU HAVE? WHERE ARE THOSE DOTS PLACED?

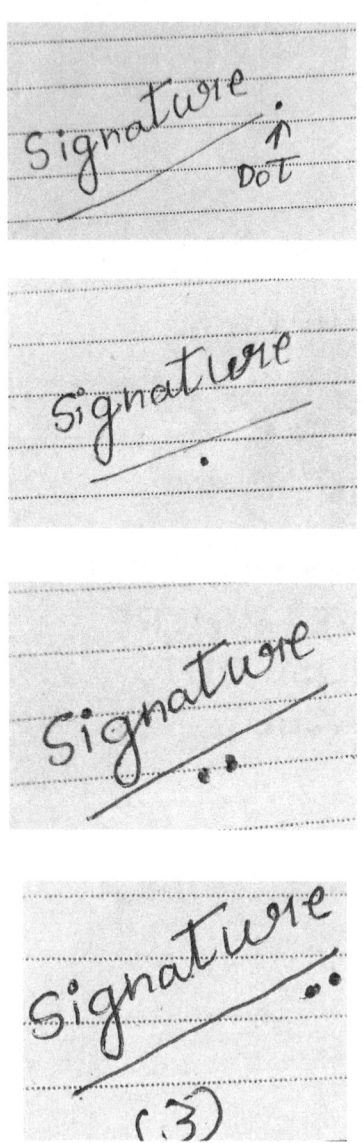

7

What Number Of Dots And It's Placement Reveals About You?

Dots can reveal lot many things yet here number of dots, placement reveals different things which is why studying both is important. You can know:

- If writer is someone who is open about his public or private life or both
- You can get to know if a writer is going to trust you directly or is going to verify.
- Dots is an interesting topic and you can say more famous as many people have asked me about dots & it's meaning
- There are various types of dots such as Single Dot, Double Dots with placements, Dot After Signature
- We'll study all!

DOT AT END

3 Dots After Signature

68] LOOK AND ANALYZE

HOW TO FIND?

- If Any Signature have 1 or more than 1 dot "after the signature" then writer fall under this category

WHAT IT INDICATES?

- It indicates impulse coming to an end, they want to say that now the conversation has ended.
- They have distrust in future
- Also these writers need verification before trusting.
- So if one of your friend sign like this then they will try to verify what you are saying most of time before accepting it.
- It is one of the common trait, you will find many people signing like this
- More the number of dots more the verification they need. Not an ideal trait

WHO SIGN LIKE THIS?

My Friend Avi

69] LOOK AND ANALYZE

1 DOT BELOW SIGN

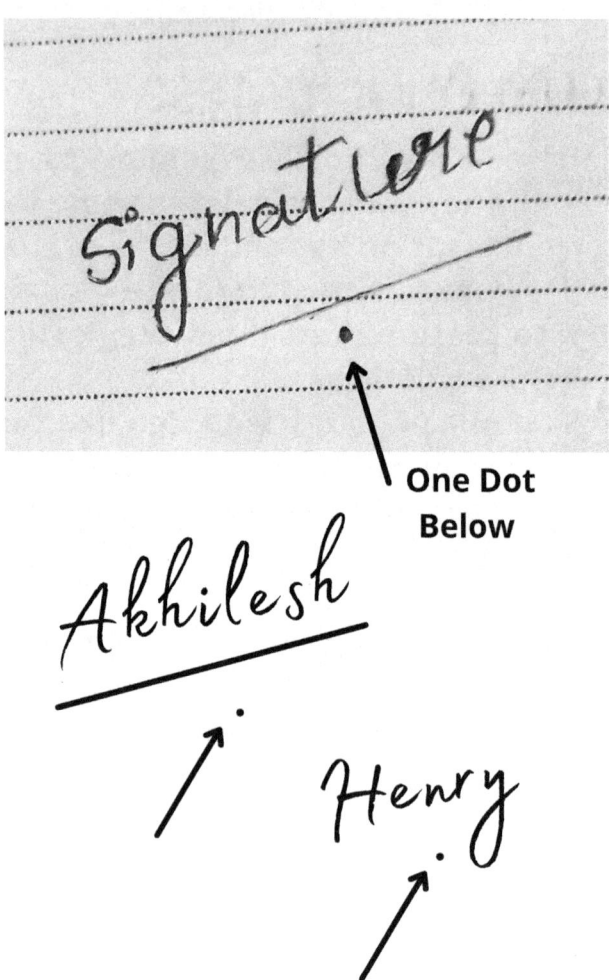

One Dot
Below

HOW TO FIND?

- A signature where "Only 1 Dot" is present "Below" the name fall under this category

WHAT IT INDICATES?

- Writers here are watchful about things.
- They are often vigilant in nature
- These writers also like to be recognized or remembered for work they have done, they are trying to convey a message that people should know who they are, what they have done
- They give careful attention to a particular problem or situation and are able to notice any change
- Not found in most signatures

WHO SIGN LIKE THIS?

Check your social circle and find if anyone sign like this

---

2 DOT BELOW SIGN

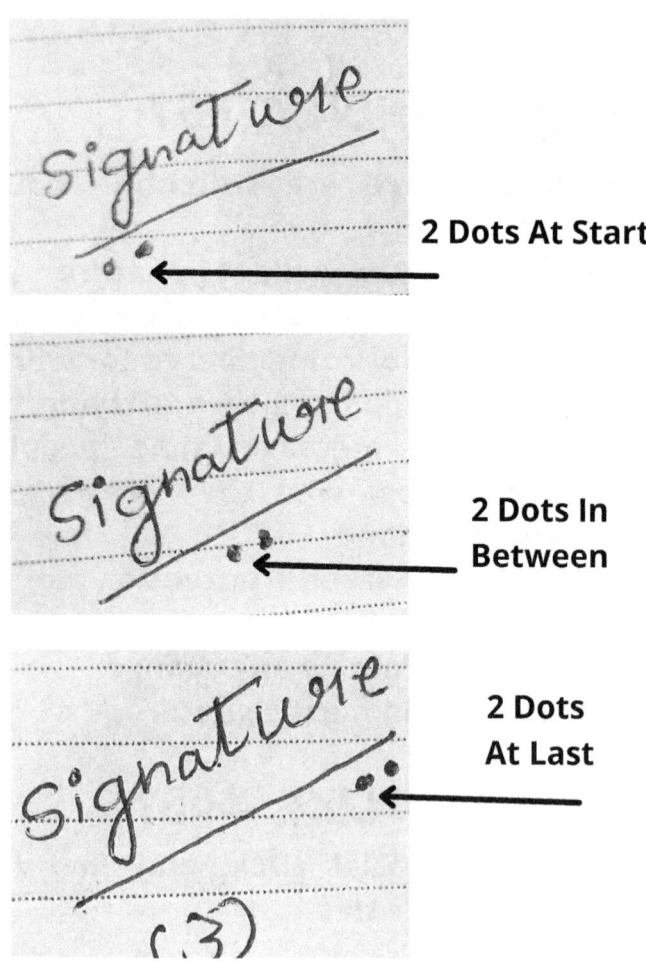

2 Dots At Start

2 Dots In Between

2 Dots At Last

72] LOOK AND ANALYZE

HOW TO FIND?

- Sign where "Only 2 Dots" are present below name are part of this trait
- Here placement too matters

WHAT IT INDICATES?

- You will find this type in many actors, actresses signatures.
- Writers are willing to get directed by others.
- Now they are also stubborn in nature so they don't just change their opinions
- For position/placement of dots, left side (Fig:1) indicates family person who is more open about his private life, right side (Fig:3) indicates more extrovert person (More open about public life), middle side (Fig:2) indicates balanced person (Both)

WHO SIGN LIKE THIS?

Amitabh Bachchan, Shahrukh Khan, Salman Khan

SIZE

WELL IN SIGNATURE SIZE DOES MATTER!

75] LOOK AND ANALYZE

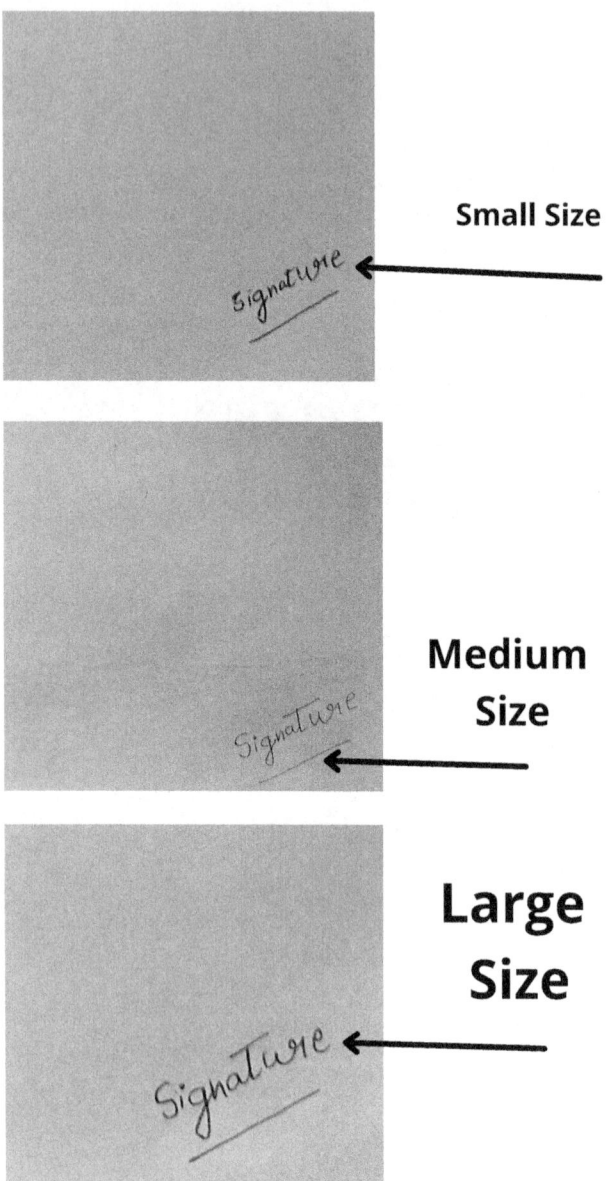

Small Size

Medium Size

Large Size

8

Your Sign Size Also Reveals Many Things About You!

- Signature size is one of the first things we notice.
- Just like number of underlines this is also a easiest trait to find
- It can help you know how much confident a writer is socially & how much open he/she will be in front of others.
- In short, it tells how you feel about yourself and the world around you.
- There are 3 types of signatures: Small size, Medium Size, Large Size
- Ideally just like handwriting size here too you can get to know if writer is comfortable interacting with others, are they introvert or extrovert

77] LOOK AND ANALYZE

SMALL SIZE

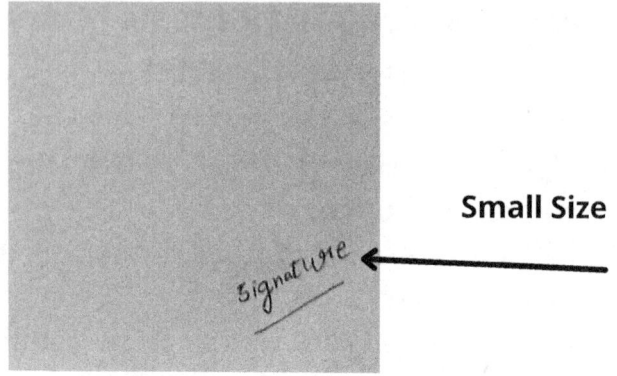

Small Size

Akhilesh

Alice

Smith

Jones

78] LOOK AND ANALYZE

HOW TO FIND?

- By just looking at sample you must get the idea as practically you will not try to measure each sign by cm right? As some samples will be a digital image

WHAT IT INDICATES?

- Small sign indicates low self-esteem, confidence levels.
- On positive side, they have good focus and tend to do few things in a perfect way
- These people may get bullied by others as they don't just stand up for themselves so it's better to increase the size
- Socially these people are not that interactive and have some shyness
- Not an Ideal Trait to have!

WHO SIGN LIKE THIS?

Shy People, Introverts

MEDIUM SIZE

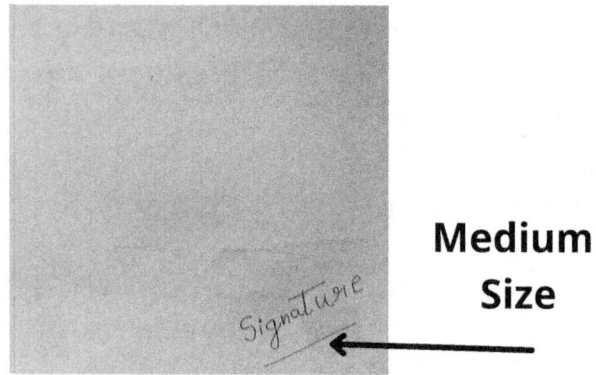

Medium
Size

Akhilesh

Alice

**Same sign examples
size are increased. You
can compare these
signs with small size
samples**

Smith

Jones

HOW TO FIND?

- For small size you need to put some effort to zoom in and here you can see the sign without putting much effort

WHAT IT INDICATES?

- Medium size sign shows balance, modesty.
- In public they are ok being recognized as well not being recognized
- It also indicates good self-image, confidence level
- Ideal sign size to have

WHO SIGN LIKE THIS?

Ambiverts or people who are comfortable being alone as well as around people

81] LOOK AND ANALYZE

LARGE SIZE

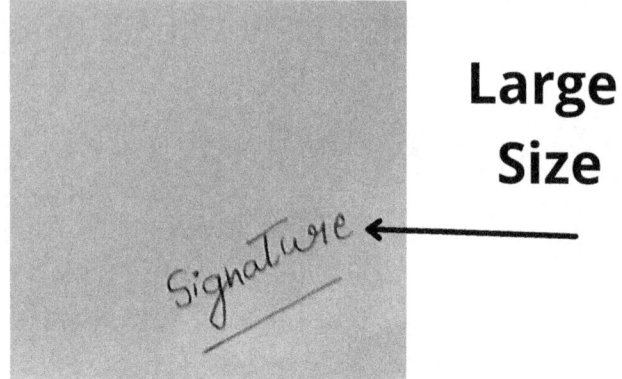

Large Size

Signature

Akhilesh

Alice

Same sign size is increased. You can compare these signs with small, medium size samples

Smith

Jones

82] LOOK AND ANALYZE

HOW TO FIND?

- Here sign is bigger than normal size sometimes you may need to zoom out a little

WHAT IT INDICATES?

- Why do we write something in large size? To get attention right? Similarly here too people who like & want attention sign like this
- They have high confidence levels yet too much large size shows overconfidence
- These people want to do many things in different fields
- People oriented, outgoing individual
- They don't settle for less

WHO SIGN LIKE THIS?

Extroverts yet you also need to look at handwriting

DIRECTION

WHICH DIRECTION DO YOU FOLLOW? UPWARDS OR DOWNWARDS OR STRAIGHT?

85] LOOK AND ANALYZE

Signature
(Upward)

Signature

Signature

9

All About Directions!

- Direction can help you know how writer is feeling at the moment like is he/she feeling optimistic or is depressed.
- You can also find if he/she likes recognition or don't like being in front as a leader
- Very Easy to analyze, I believe this may be the first trait you analyze
- There are 3 types of common directions:

1] Upward Direction
2] Straight Direction
3] Downward Direction

- If you have studied about baselines in handwriting analysis then you can use same concept here

---

UPWARD DIRECTION

Signature

(Upward)

Akhilesh

Bob

Jeff

Willow

88] LOOK AND ANALYZE

HOW TO FIND?

- If you find any signature that goes in upward direction then that writer is part of this trait

WHAT IT INDICATES?

- Where do you look when you feel happy, optimistic? In upward direction right?
- Similarly people who sign like this are optimistic in nature.
- They like to be in front as a leader so you will often find these writers leading teams, family, groups
- Like attention of others & being recognized by others for the work they have done.
- Ambitious, Forward thinking individual.
- Many public speakers, successful people sign like this.

WHO SIGN LIKE THIS?

Amitabh Bachchan, Cristiano Ronaldo, Shahrukh Khan

89] LOOK AND ANALYZE

STRAIGHT DIRECTION

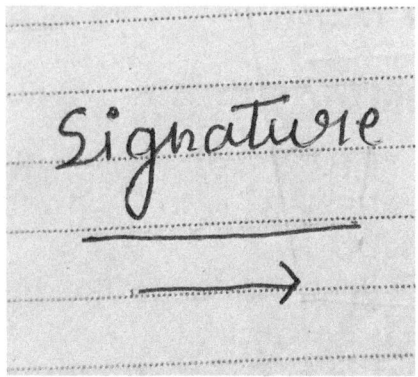

All Signatures are at 0 Degree

Akhilesh

Bob

Jeff

Willow

HOW TO FIND?

- Signature which is straight or at 0 degree fall under this category

WHAT IT INDICATES?

- Writing exactly straight is little difficult on blank page right? The reason people who sign like this have high control
- Now these people focus on small details, go for perfection
- Balance is something they value the most!
- Instead of being in front they like working behind the scenes
- They don't push themselves too much
- They don't think too much about attention, recognition

WHO SIGN LIKE THIS?

People who are working as a stuntmen, assistants, makeup artist or Entrepreneurs who don't like much attention. Eg- Ratan Tata

---

DOWNWARD DIRECTION

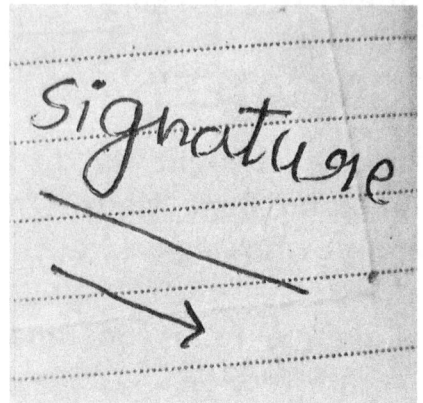

Akhilesh

Bob

Jeff

Willow

HOW TO FIND?

- Signature going in downward direction

WHAT IT INDICATES?

- Imagine you are feeling very sad, depressed due to some incident. Now in which direction are you looking in? In downward direction right?
- Same happens here, writer is feeling stress about something henceforth it's going down
- It also indicates lack of energy, insecurity
- Upward sign people are optimistic while downward sign people are pessimistic
- Once in a while you find this trait as it is not common in signatures

WHO SIGN LIKE THIS?

Stressed, Depressed individuals

Slants

WELL DO YOU TAKE
EMOTIONAL
DECISIONS OR
LOGICAL DECISIONS?

95] LOOK AND ANALYZE

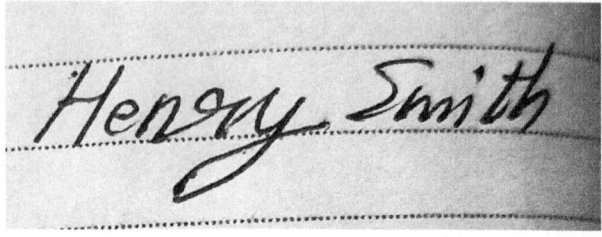

Right Side Slant (Signature is tilted on right side!)

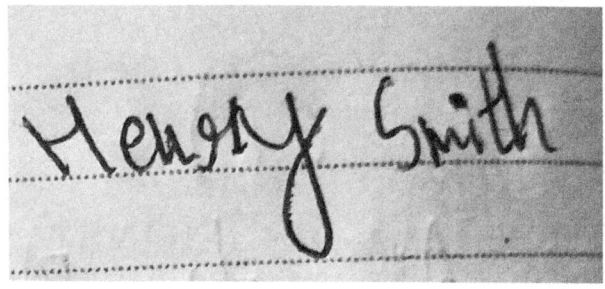

Left Side Slant (Signature is tilted on left side!)

10

Slants

- Apart from upward, straight, downward direction there is also 2 more types of directions which in Graphology are known as slants.
- Rightward and leftward slant can help you know if an individual is a private person or is a more sociable one.
- You can also know if he/she shares their emotions with others or not
- Just like direction, slant is also an easy trait to find out
- Most of the time you will find straight direction/slant only yet still having knowledge is important
- Writer who have straight slant (90 degree handwriting like this font) are logical people in nature who don't make emotional decisions

RIGHT SLANT

Right Side Slant (Signature is tilted on right side!)

Jeff

Bob

Akhilesh

Muhammad Ali

98] LOOK AND ANALYZE

HOW TO FIND?

- Here the signature letters are tilted on right side
- Any signature where angle is less than 90 Degree (Acute Angle)

WHAT IT INDICATES?

- These people are sociable people and are friendly in nature
- Many creative people, inventors, actors, actresses, poets have this type of slant.
- Writers here are emotional as well yet it also helps them in connecting with people, understanding others.
- They are able to visualize things more clearly and are able to connect emotions to it.

WHO SIGN LIKE THIS?

Muhammed Ali, Albert Einstein, Benjamin Franklin

LEFT SLANT

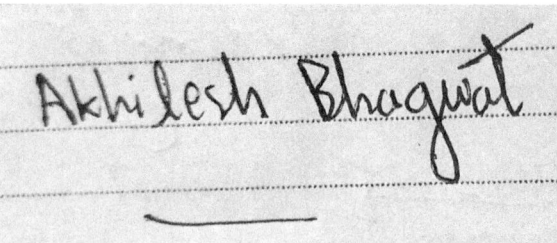

Left Side Slant (Signature is tilted on left side!)

HOW TO FIND?

- Here the signature letters are tilted on left side
- Any signature where angle is more than 90 Degree (Obtuse Angle)

WHAT IT INDICATES?

- These writers are reserved in nature and are private individuals
- They will not just get involved with people unless they know them
- Now they are polite in nature yet will not just share their feelings, emotions or even any information about them with others
- This behavior could be due to past, childhood as they may have not got anyone who they can share their feelings with in past so now they still believe same

WHO SIGN LIKE THIS?

People who don't share their emotions, feelings with others

Placement

DO YOU SIGN ON LEFT
SIDE OR ON RIGHT
SIDE OR IN MIDDLE?

103] LOOK AND ANALYZE

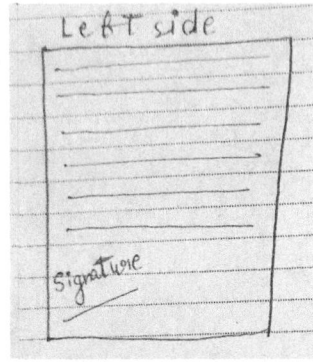

Left Side

Middle Side

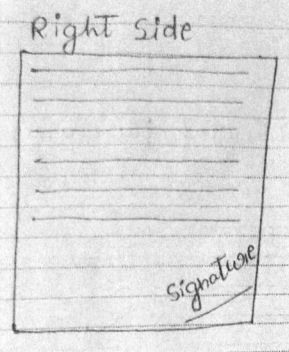

Right Side

11

Placements - On which side do you sign in?

- In Graphology, writing from left to right indicates going from past to future.
- A placement in signature help us know the mindset of the writer, you can know if he is living in past or is future oriented.
- There are 3 types of placement:

1] Right Side placement
2] Middle Side Placement
3] Left Side Placement

- This is also one of easiest trait to find as you can instantly find it
- Normally to find placement you also need to have handwriting as well. So both samples are needed where handwriting is at top & sign at bottom in same page
- Also remember to ask writer if they also sign like this as sometimes they may have signed on left side since their job says so

LEFT SIDE PLACEMENT

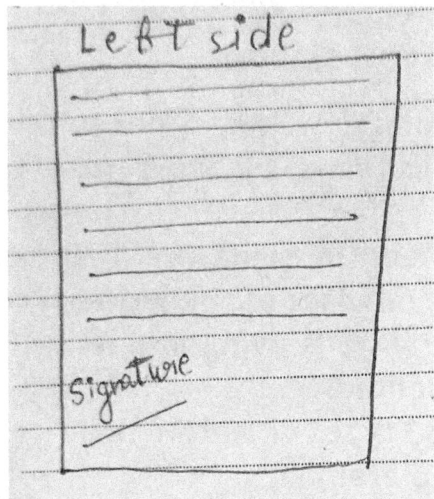

106] LOOK AND ANALYZE

HOW TO FIND?

- Signature is placed on left side of the page...simple!

WHAT IT INDICATES?

- In Graphology left side indicates past.
- Here writer is thinking, living in past rather than moving on
- Due to trauma they have unknown fear as well which stops them from moving forward
- Not an ideal trait
- Remember context matters as sometimes they may have this habit due to their work, job

WHO SIGN LIKE THIS?

Past Thinkers

MIDDLE SIDE PLACEMENT

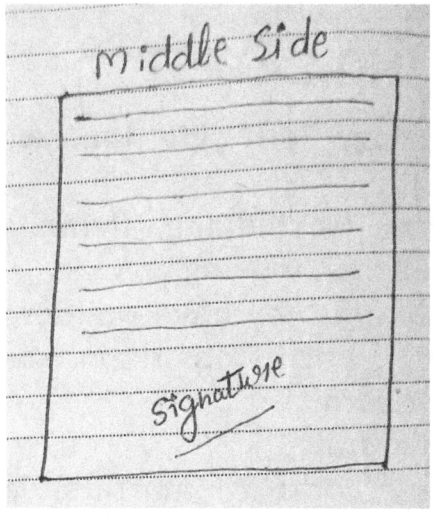

HOW TO FIND?

- Signature is placed on middle side of the page

WHAT IT INDICATES?

- If left side shows past and right shows future then what would middle side show? Present right?
- Writer here likes attention of people as he likes to stand in middle rather than on corner.
- These people also want to be dominant, to be seen as the leader.
- Many actors, actresses have this type of sign.
- They also tend to focus more on living in the moment.

WHO SIGN LIKE THIS?

People who want attention and like to live in the moment

RIGHT SIDE PLACEMENT

HOW TO FIND?

- Signature is placed on right side of the page

WHAT IT INDICATES?

- I believe now you already know about right side. Right side shows future!
- So here writer is moving in forward direction as we start writing from left side and go towards right it shows we are going forward from past
- They are ambitious people in nature
- Also they don't think too much about past
- Ideal trait to have!
- Yet remember to never overdo or go too much in right direction as it indicates impulsive nature

WHO SIGN LIKE THIS?

Future Oriented Individual

Pressure

HIGH ENERGY OR LOW ENERGY!

113] LOOK AND ANALYZE

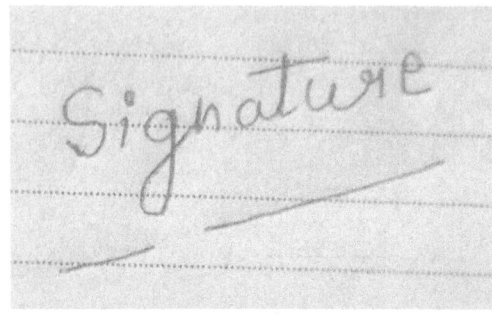

Light Pressure

Heavy Pressure

12

All About Pressure

- A writer's energy levels are determined with pressure in handwriting analysis,
- Here in sign too you can know how writer want others to see him as.
- For eg- As an energetic person or the opposite one.
- Similarly you can also know aggressiveness, empathy levels as well
- To find pressure you need to have a sample which is written with blue/black ball pen. Blue works best
- Pencil, Sketch Pen, Gel Pen, Markers, Ink Pen cannot help you know the pressure.
- Also blue/black are best than any other colors
- Sample must be original, it must not be a scanned one

HIGH PRESSURE

Signature

Akhilesh

Sachin

Bill

Jane

___
HOW TO FIND?

- Signature looks darker or bold

___
WHAT IT INDICATES?

- Remember to check both handwriting, sign
- Here writer want others to see him as an energetic person.
- Someone who can do lot of tasks in a single day
- Writer here is aggressive in nature
- Gives 100% to every work they do
- Normally we don't look at this trait for only signature yet it's better to have some knowledge

___
WHO SIGN LIKE THIS?

People who want others to see them as an energetic person

117] LOOK AND ANALYZE

LOW PRESSURE

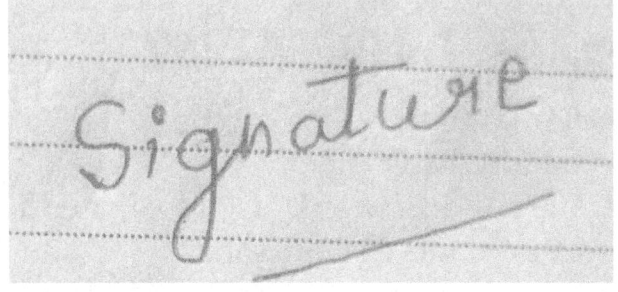

Akhilesh

Sachin

Bill

Jane

HOW TO FIND?

- **Signature looks light**

WHAT IT INDICATES?

- **Light or low pressure indicates low energy levels.**
- **These people are lazy in nature and will not move easily**
- **On positive side, they are compassionate and show empathy towards others**
- **They understand others**
- **Prone to diseases due to low immunity levels**

WHO SIGN LIKE THIS?

People who are lazy, less energetic

Speed

NERVOUS OR CONFIDENT?

121] LOOK AND ANALYZE

Signed With High Speed

Signed With Low Speed

Can you find difference between both?
No Right? Henceforth always make
writer sign in front of you if you want to
analyze this trait

13

Speed

- Speed is the trait you may not be able to see unless writer signs in front of you.
- Yet it does reveal writer's ability of keeping patience, going for perfection, confidence level as well.
- There are 2 main types of speed,

1]Slow speed

2]Fast speed.

- You may not be able to look at this trait at all times.
- Now you can also find nervousness of a person with this.
- If you are an HR then it can help you know how much nervous the person you are interviewing is
- Context matters here as well so you need to ask writer if they sign like this normally.

123] LOOK AND ANALYZE

FAST SPEED

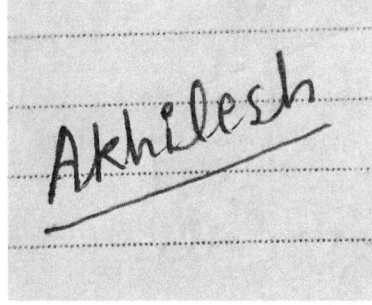

Signed In Under 3 Seconds

124] LOOK AND ANALYZE

HOW TO FIND?

- Writer signs in within 3 seconds

WHAT IT INDICATES?

- These writers want to get things done as quickly as possible.
- They are impatient as well.
- Also they don't like waiting too much or even thinking too much.
- Sometimes you will also find a nervous person signing like this.
- Look at other traits as well
- Remember writer must sign in front of you!

WHO SIGN LIKE THIS?

People who want to do things as fast as possible

SLOW SPEED

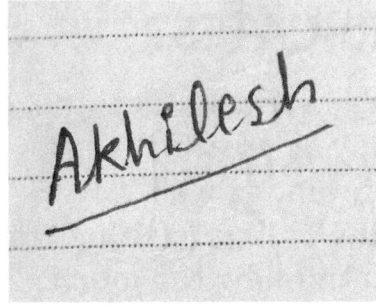

It Takes More Than 5 Seconds To Sign In

HOW TO FIND?

- It Takes More Than 5 Seconds To Sign In

WHAT IT INDICATES?

- "Calm is the superpower" you may have often heard this lot of times and writers here are calm in nature
- They are able to get most things done not quickly yet surely.
- The reason they are able to achieve their goals
- Writing at own pace indicates good self-confidence
- If it takes more than usual time to sign then writer may be a lazy person

WHO SIGN LIKE THIS?

People who like to work, walk at their own pace

Negative Signatures

AVOID THESE SIGNATURES AT ALL COST!

129] LOOK AND ANALYZE

Name   Akhilesh
Name cut
(cut through sigh)
X

Signature
(←

Tony

@Bhagwat

Signature
cut

extended
Signature ←

Henry Coupe
↓
Drop

(2)

Henry Singh
Too much extended
loops

AKHILESH BHAGWAT

14

Negative Signatures

- There is no perfect signature even I don't have perfect one & no one can have it as every positive trait comes with a negative trait.
- Just like Ying-Yang circle everything is balanced
- Now you may be thinking if nothing is perfect then "why are we learning these avoid traits as they too have negative in it and other positive traits too have some negative in it?"
- Well it's always better to at least have some gain and some loss than having full loss.
- The traits we are studying only have negative meanings and that is the reason we are studying and avoiding them

SUICIDE SIGNATURE

~~Name~~   ~~Akhilesh~~

Name cut
(cut through sign)

X

HOW TO FIND?

- Writer cuts his/her name in the signature

WHAT IT INDICATES?

- It look like here writer hates themselves and henceforth are cutting their names, it's like cutting themselves
- You can find this type of sign in many suicide notes
- Now just because someone is signing like this doesn't mean they are going to do suicide instantly as some times it would have been a mistake so do ask them to sign some more times. If still the sign looks same then do talk with them and give them support. You may save someone's life

WHO SIGN LIKE THIS?

People who are feeling lot of stress

TRACEBACK SIGNATURE

134] LOOK AND ANALYZE

HOW TO FIND?

- Here underline gets extended from last letter and goes in leftward direction or downward direction

WHAT IT INDICATES?

- This type of sign is known as Traceback Sign as underline goes in backward direction
- Writer here lives in past and is not able to let go things be it failures, disappointments.
- Unable to make firm future decisions
- You will find many people signing like this as it's a common type signature

WHO SIGN LIKE THIS?

People who are living in past

135] LOOK AND ANALYZE

CAMOUFLAGE SIGN

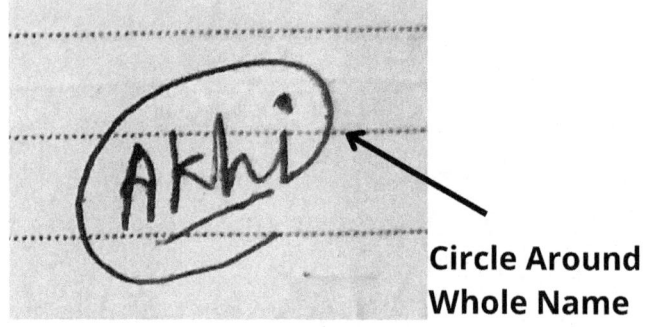

Circle Around Whole Name

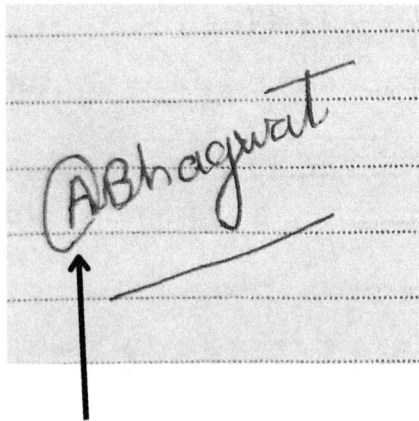

Circle Only Around First Letter

HOW TO FIND?

- Circle is formed either around a particular letter or whole name which could be only first name or last name or full name

WHAT IT INDICATES?

- To understand this, think circle like a bubble where writer protects himself/herself emotionally from outside influence.
- So they are trying to protect their emotions
- Now it is a sign of anxiety, inner withdrawal from social relationships
- Overthinking, Self-blame are the problems they face a lot.
- They are over protective & have self-limiting beliefs.
- Another very common sign type

WHO SIGN LIKE THIS?

People who keep their emotions inside instead of sharing up

LOWER ZONE CUT SIGN

HOW TO FIND?

- The Underline cuts letter y, g, j or any other lower zone letters

WHAT IT INDICATES?

- Writer has been pushing herself/himself due to excessive work.
- If something wrong happens then these people tend to blame themselves without understanding just like circle sign
- Lower zones or y, j, g, f are all about relationships so cutting it is not good for your social, romantic relationships as well as finances
- To fix this draw the underline below whole signature even below y, g, j

WHO SIGN LIKE THIS?

People who are pushing themselves more than needed, workaholics

BAD FINISHERS

extended

signature ←

Akhilesh

**Last Letter
Extended**

HOW TO FIND?

- The last letter is extended forming a line

WHAT IT INDICATES?

- As you can observe, sign is completed yet writer still wants to extend
- These writers tend to push a lot at start yet as the finishing line comes near they tend to either give up or keep procrastinating or lose motivation
- To fix it, just don't extend the last letter
- If you have problem completing things or sign like this then above fix could be a good change to do. (You need to change handwriting as well)

WHO SIGN LIKE THIS?

Bad Finishers

DROP AT LAST

Henry Coupe
↓
Drop

Signature
↓
Drop

142] LOOK AND ANALYZE

HOW TO FIND?

- End letters or just a letter drops down

WHAT IT INDICATES?

- As we have studied earlier, in Graphology upward direction shows optimism while downward direction shows stress, depression
- Writer here is feeling depressed as letters are going downward
- It is a sign of emotional conflict.
- It is also a red flag just like name cut which is found in suicide notes
- Talk with the writer if you find this trait in their signature as they may need some help.
- Sometimes you will find sign going upwards and at last it drop down. It shows writer is trying to be optimistic yet the stress is still there. They need more motivation

WHO SIGN LIKE THIS?

People who are feeling stress

SCRIBBLED SIGN

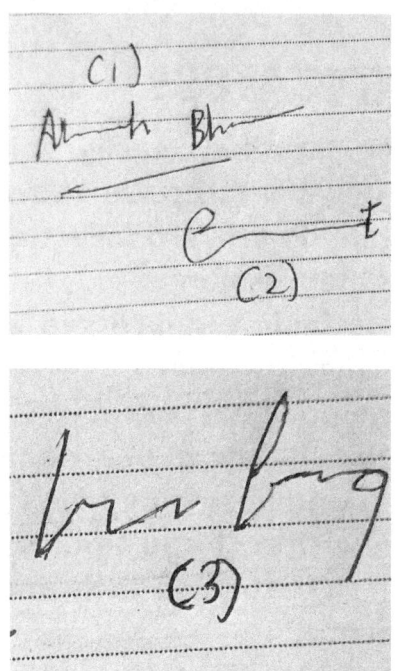

144] LOOK AND ANALYZE

HOW TO FIND?

- Sign looks like a scribble.
- Scribble - Remember when we test a new pen? We just scribble a little to see if ink is present or not

WHAT IT INDICATES?

- Normally we scribble when we are casual and don't care much of what we are writing
- Same is here writer doesn't take their signature seriously
- These people are careless in nature and always seem to be in rush
- They may have fast minds
- Don't take responsibility for their actions instead blame others
- Now context matters here as most doctors have casual sign similar to this yet their official sign is different so focus on official one

WHO SIGN LIKE THIS?

Careless Individuals

ALL CAPITALS

All capitals

All capital

AKHILESH BHAGWAT

JOHNSMITH

ODIN

CONOR

146] LOOK AND ANALYZE

HOW TO FIND?

- All letters in the signature are CAPITAL!

WHAT IT INDICATES?

- Have you observed "BUY NOW", "ENROLL NOW", "%OFF", "DANGER" all these texts are always capital. You know why? Importance, they are showing us that they are important
- Similarly here too writer is trying to show others that they are superior to others and are important
- They have some insecurities, weaknesses & low esteem which makes them think like this
- Impressing others is one of the main goal for them.
- They try to show others that they are proud of who they are

WHO SIGN LIKE THIS?

People who want to feel important

147] LOOK AND ANALYZE

BIG y, g, j LOOPS

Henry Singh

Too much extended loops

148] LOOK AND ANALYZE

HOW TO FIND?

- The letter y or g or j loops are too bigger in size

WHAT IT INDICATES?

- You can consider loop as bag, so bigger the bag more the money writer craves.
- Letter y, g, j are all about relationships, sex drives, finances, lower body
- Too much bigger loop indicates materialism.
- Writer here craves for materials, desires for which they may break any rules
- It happens mainly because writer's cravings are not fulfilled.
- Ideally it's important to have balance loop

WHO SIGN LIKE THIS?

Materialistic people

149] LOOK AND ANALYZE

CLAWS

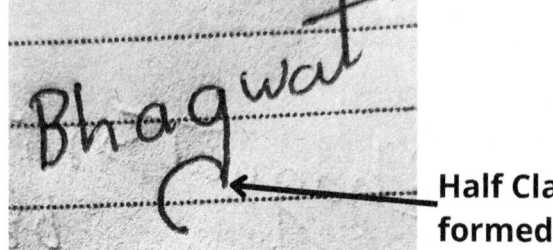

Half Claw is formed

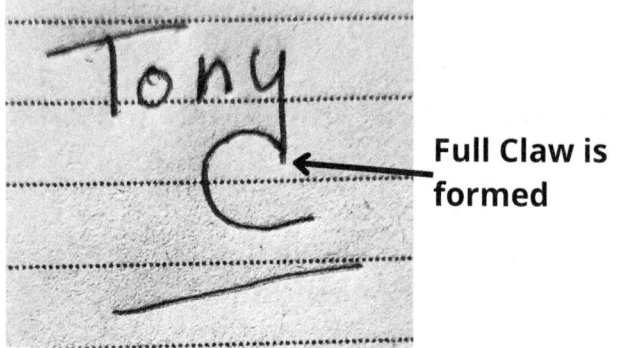

Full Claw is formed

150] LOOK AND ANALYZE

HOW TO FIND?

- A claw is formed which is mostly found in y, g, j yet you can also find it in other letters as well like letter A

WHAT IT INDICATES?

- These writers feel guilty about the image they are projecting in front of others.
- Commonly found in letter y, g, f, j
- Often you will find this trait in people who had very tough childhood.
- Higher the Claw more the guilt a writer is feeling.
- Replace the claw with complete y loop

WHO SIGN LIKE THIS?

Tony Robbins

BIG INITIALS AND VERY SMALL LETTERS

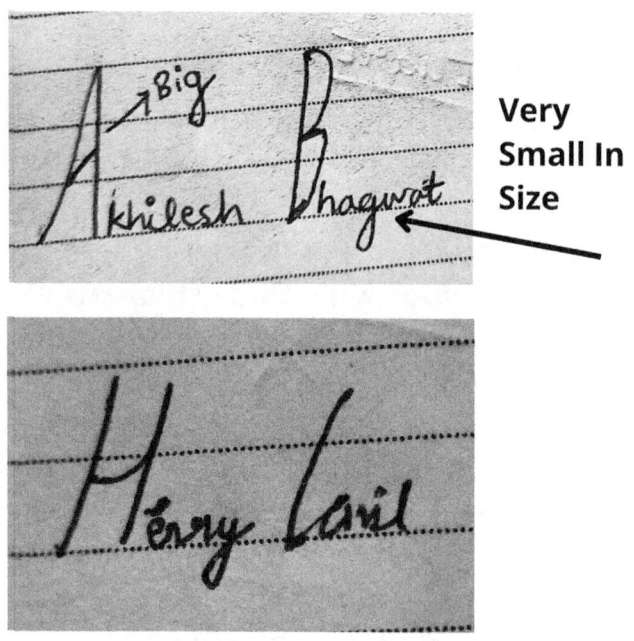

HOW TO FIND?

- Here the initial letters are very big while other small letters are very small in size

WHAT IT INDICATES?

- Too big initials indicates very high ego and these people have lot of pride.
- They will keep talking about how great they are, their work and achievements in a very overly manner.
- They believe that they are superior due to which they become arrogant with others
- Due to this nature other people try to avoid/hate them and the writer don't even realize this and still keep same behavior of bragging.

WHO SIGN LIKE THIS?

Overly Confident People, Very high EGO

LAST NAME CUT

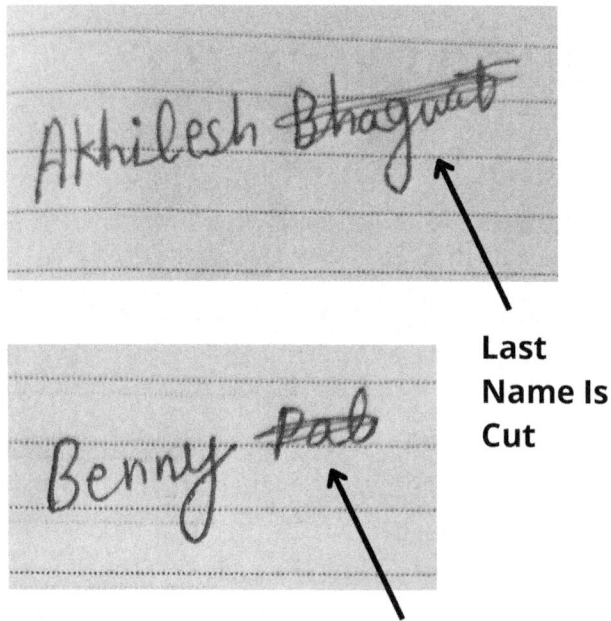

Last
Name Is
Cut

154]LOOK AND ANALYZE

HOW TO FIND?

- First Name looks clear yet last name has been cut with either a line or a messy scribble

WHAT IT INDICATES?

- We have seen "The Suicide Sign" where writer cuts his/her own first name, this happens because writer hates himself/herself.
- Here too logic is same, if a person cuts their lastname then it means they have some issues with family
- If a writer is a male and have his father's last name then it means writer have some issue with his father. For married women it's issue with her husband
- Never Cut Your First Name, Last Name or any name in signature!

WHO SIGN LIKE THIS?

Writers having family issues

X-ing Signature

HOW TO FIND?

- Writer cuts y, j, g with a short line (It's not a underline) in such a way that a "x" or "+" is formed.

WHAT IT INDICATES?

- Firstly, this sign is also found in many suicide notes.
- The reason this sign type also fall under red flag signature
- Writer start signing like this after a serious loss, death of a loved one, defeat
- Sign of inner fears, depression.
- Best to avoid it
- Talk with writer if he/she is having this signature
- Again just because someone is having this sign doesn't mean they will do suicide. There could be a high stress level

WHO SIGN LIKE THIS?

Depressed People

Bonus 1: Letter Traits

LETTER TYPES IN SIGNATURES & THEIR MEANING

159] LOOK AND ANALYZE

Akhilesh

Akhilesh

Walt Disney

Akhilesh

Stuart

Akhilesh

Stuart

Tendulkar

Benjamin Franklin

15

Letter Traits

- Whatever we have studied earlier was all part of only signature analysis so in handwriting analysis you may not find the underlines or names or dots.
- Yet right now we are going to learn something which is found in both handwriting and signature analysis
- That element is letters
- Both handwriting, sign include letters and the meaning for these letters remains same for both
- We are not going to study all 26 letters and it's type instead we will have a closer look at some important letters which are t, i, m, n.

HIGH t BAR

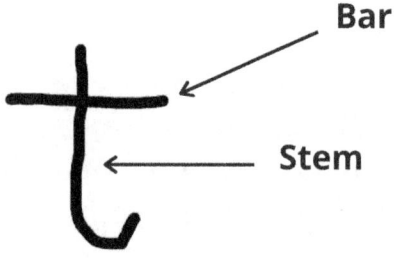

Bar

Stem

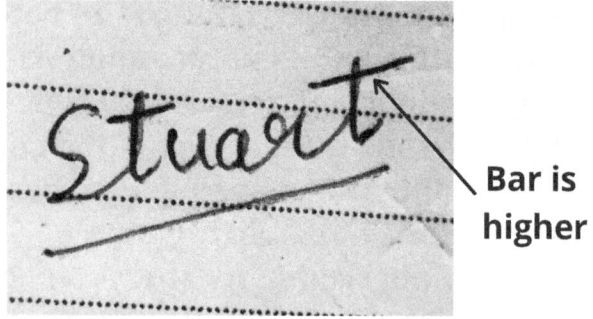

Bar is higher

___

HOW TO FIND?

- Here the bar is higher (More distance from bottom of the Stem)

___

WHAT IT INDICATES?

- High t bars indicate high esteem and confidence levels
- These writers want to be seen as someone who dream big and push themselves.
- Higher the t bar higher the confidence as well as ego
- Found in many successful people's signature as well as handwriting
- Now remember sometimes you may find high t bar in signature and low t bar in handwriting. It shows writer is faking their personality in public

___

WHO SIGN LIKE THIS?

People who want to be seen as a confident person

LOW t BAR

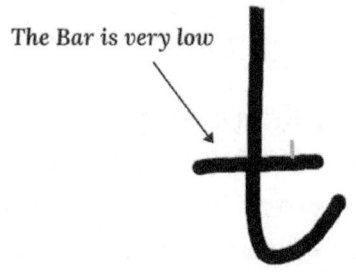

The Bar is very low

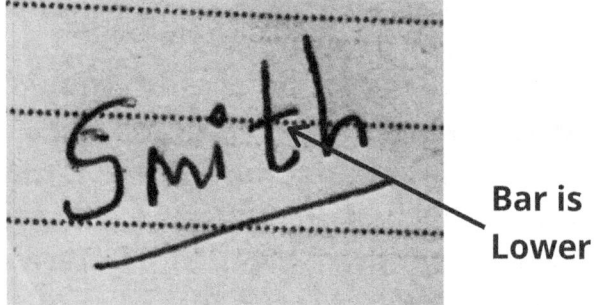

Bar is Lower

HOW TO FIND?

- Here the bar is lower (Less distance from bottom of the Stem)

WHAT IT INDICATES?

- Lower the t bar less the self-esteem a writer is having. So their self-image is not good
- Not an ideal trait to have in signature as well as in handwriting
- Change your t to high bar if you have this type of trait
- Now sometimes writer is having low confidence level in social life and that could be a reason for having this type of t

WHO SIGN LIKE THIS?

Writers having low social confidence

MIDDLE t BARS

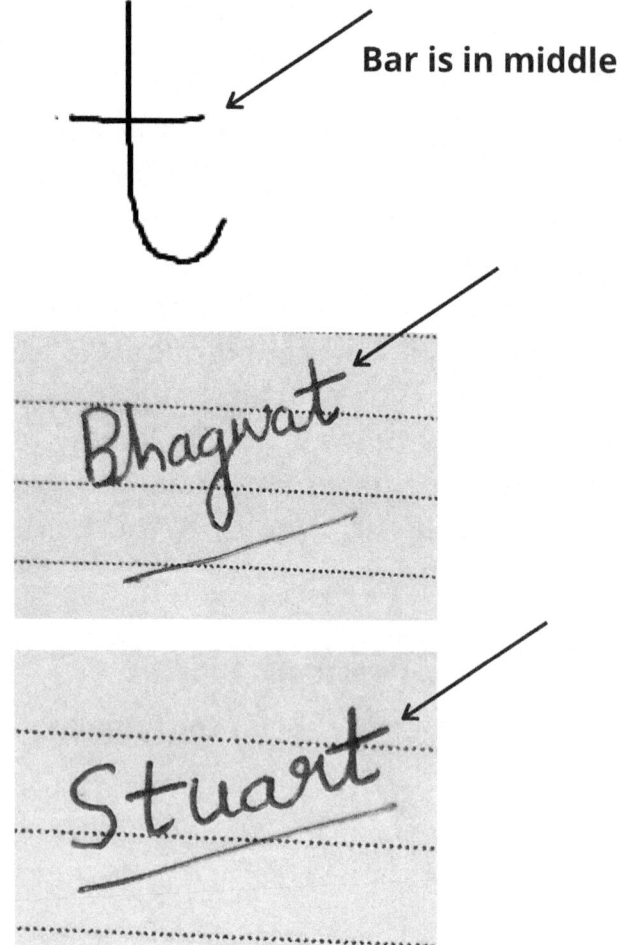

Bar is in middle

166] LOOK AND ANALYZE

HOW TO FIND?

- Here the bar is in middle

WHAT IT INDICATES?

- Writers here have balance self-esteem.
- They know who they are.
- They also don't push themselves much and tend to have balance approach towards life.
- For eg- To not dream too big and also to not be on low side
- An ideal trait as well yet high t bar is best if you want to be successful

WHO SIGN LIKE THIS?

People who have average level confidence

FAST THINKERS

Pointed

W *n*

Pointed n

A. Einstein

Tendulakar

Benjamin Franklin

HOW TO FIND?

- Letter m, n are pointed or angular

WHAT IT INDICATES?

- These writers are fast thinkers who make quick decisions.
- Mind runs constantly wanting to achieve things as fast as possible
- They are intelligent in nature and most likely to be in authority or important positions
- Remember in handwriting m, n also needs to be pointed.
- These people are always in hurry

WHO SIGN LIKE THIS?

Ratan Tata, Mukesh Ambani, Albert Einstein

SLOW THINKERS

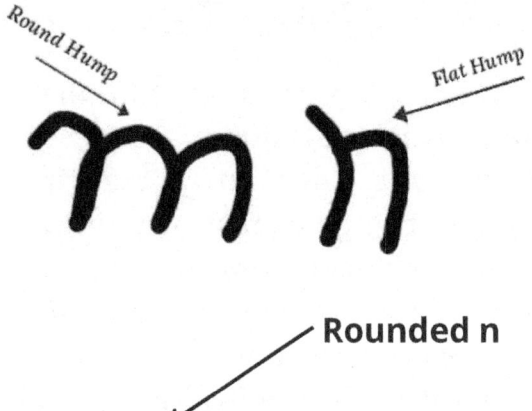

Round Hump

Flat Hump

Rounded n

A. Einstein

Tendulkar

Benjamin Franklin

HOW TO FIND?

- Letter m, n are rounded or flat

WHAT IT INDICATES?

- These writers don't rush into doing things instead they think before taking decisions, doing stuff
- They have good long-term memory
- Soft Hearted people who are able to do lot of tasks sitting at one place
- Again handwriting m, n also needs to be same
- They may take some time to learn new things yet once learned they remember it for longer time

WHO SIGN LIKE THIS?

People who have good long term memory

NO DOT IN i

Dot is missing

HOW TO FIND?

- The dot in letter "i" is missing

WHAT IT INDICATES?

- Dots are important in letter i as it tell about imagination, creativity, focus, organization.
- No dot indicates very less attention span due to which they get distracted more quickly which makes them prone to making lot of mistakes.
- They also take lot of time to get work done due to low focus.
- Always put dot in letter i

WHO SIGN LIKE THIS?

Careless individuals

DOT RIGHT ABOVE i STEM

Dot is right above stem

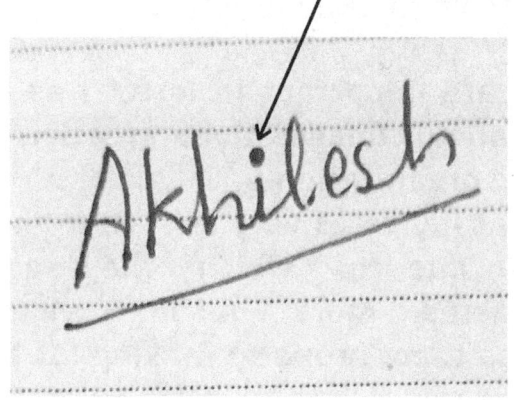

HOW TO FIND?

- The dot is present right above "i" stem

WHAT IT INDICATES?

- People here are organized in nature and like to keep things on check.
- Writers here want others to see them as a detail oriented person who focus on small details be it about what they have dressed up, grooming, environment, people, nature, etc.
- They are the people who will complete things on time, notice the things which others are unable to do.

WHO SIGN LIKE THIS?

Detail oriented writers

HIGH DOT IN i

Dot is placed at higher position

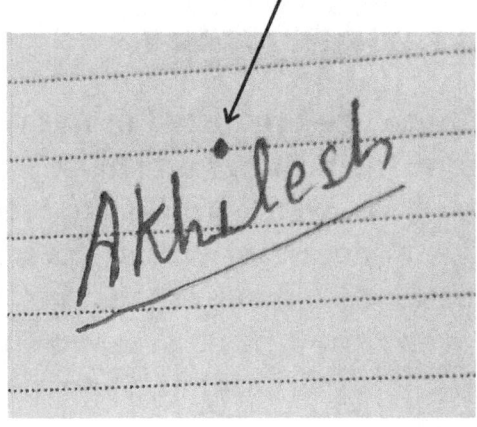

HOW TO FIND?

- Dot is placed at higher position

WHAT IT INDICATES?

- These writers have very good imagination.
- Higher the dot more the imagination, creativity level they have.
- Here people want others to see them as a creative person who like to dream, create, innovate. (They are not childish in nature)
- Many top inventors, even innovators, book writers, bloggers, artists have this type of trait.

WHO SIGN LIKE THIS?

Writers having high imagination

BUBBLE DOT IN i

Dot is placed at higher position

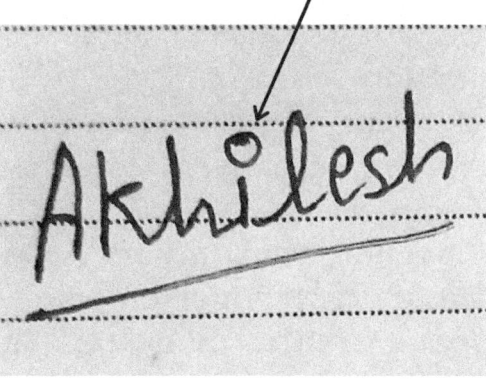

HOW TO FIND?

- Dot placed is empty circle or look like letter "o"

WHAT IT INDICATES?

- If you write like this then you have very good imagination power and creativity inside yourself.
- Writers here want the world to see them as a child or immature person who have childish behavior.
- You will often see these people wearing dress like a very young person.
- These people can be found in career which need creativity/innovation like architecture, film industry, poet, cartoon.

WHO SIGN LIKE THIS?

Writers who have childish behavior and very good imagination, Walt Disney

EXTRA: CELEBRITY SIGN

Amitabh Bachchan

Brad Pitt

HOW TO FIND?

- Initials are more bigger than small letters. (Not very large)

WHAT IT INDICATES?

- Writers here have pride about themselves.
- Larger the capital more the pride (Too large is not good as we have studied earlier)
- Creative people, want to have prominent place in public
- They are willing to get directed by others, the reason many actors, actresses have this type of signature

WHO SIGN LIKE THIS?

Shahrukh Khan, Salman Khan

Bonus 2: Advance Concepts!

CONDITIONS

183] LOOK AND ANALYZE

Today is a good day, I am happy & grateful to universe for everything. Thank You!

Jatin Bhoir

My Name is Henry Smith. I am 22 yrs old living in California, USA. Thank You For your response

Henry Smith

I have very imaginative mind sometimes I am emotional get that's okay, human in nature

David Bose

Hello there, Would you like to listen to my voice? I am a singer by heart & artist by passion.

Rahul Iyer

mickey mouse is my fav cartoon, I can watch this course, cartoon whole day both are my fav.

Amey Kale

Who stole my cheese? I want it back. I will eat you all if you don't give it back!

meow cat

16

Different Conditions

- Conditions is another advance concept in signature analysis.
- Handwriting indicates private persona while sign indicates public one.
- Now you will often find people who are different in private and different in public, condition can help you know who is real and who is fake.
- It can also help you find many interesting things about someone
- For Eg- Someone maybe very confident, talkative at home yet in social or outside home they are very quiet and less confident. This can be found out which is amazing
- Conditions can help you in finding someone's whole personality as you look at handwriting as well as signature.
- Explanation here are more short!
- "Little" means just a bit, "Very" means too much

SIGN LITTLE LARGE, HANDWRITING SMALL

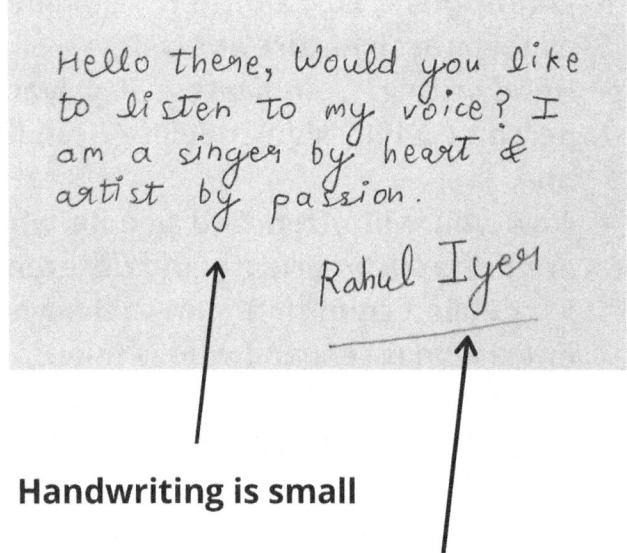

Hello there, Would you like
to listen to my voice? I
am a singer by heart &
artist by passion.

Rahul Iyer

Handwriting is small

**Signature Is Little Large
(Look at l, y, r in
handwriting as well in sign
you can find the difference)**

186] LOOK AND ANALYZE

HOW TO FIND?

- Signature letter size is little Larger than Handwriting letters

WHAT IT INDICATES?

- Ideally your sign size must be little larger than your handwriting
- It indicates healthy confidence in public.
- It's ok if you have signature which is just little larger than handwriting

WHO SIGN LIKE THIS?

Balanced People

SIGN VERY LARGE, HANDWRITING SMALL

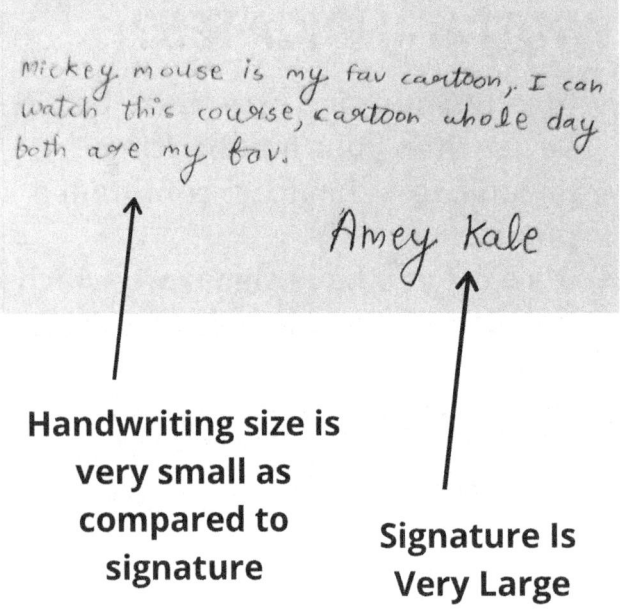

Handwriting size is very small as compared to signature

Signature Is Very Large

Now here Handwriting is small doesn't mean handwriting size is small only as handwriting size could be medium or large yet signature size is always more larger than that

188] LOOK AND ANALYZE

HOW TO FIND?

- Signature letter size is very Large compared to handwriting

WHAT IT INDICATES?

- Writer here want other's attention, it's like screaming to be seen.
- Now here a person feel small in private yet in public he is trying to be bigger to overcome his feelings
- Overdoing of something is not good
- This writer often brag about how good they are, about intelligence/skills or other things
- They may appear as very important or confident yet in reality they are not
- Always keep sign size just a little large than handwriting yet not very large

WHO SIGN LIKE THIS?

People who try to be someone who they are not

SIGN LITTLE SMALL, HANDWRITING LARGE

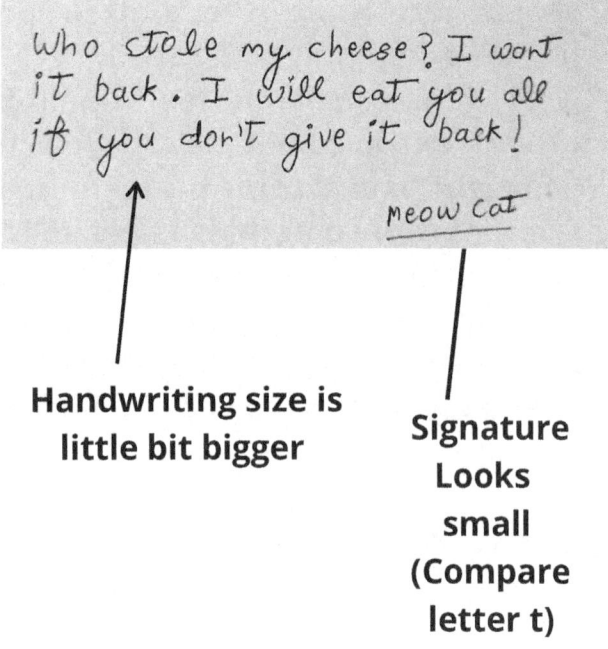

Who stole my cheese? I want it back. I will eat you all if you don't give it back!

Meow Cat

Handwriting size is little bit bigger

Signature Looks small (Compare letter t)

HOW TO FIND?

- Signature letter size is little bit small compared to handwriting

WHAT IT INDICATES?

- Writers here are insecure about themselves
- So it may happen that he/she may be very confident or even good in private life yet in public situations he/she lose that.
- They are shy, reserved type people
- Most likely work in behind the scenes rather than in front on stage. For eg- Back Stage Crew rather than the main Speaker

WHO SIGN LIKE THIS?

People who are quiet in public yet at home they are talkitive

SIGN VERY SMALL, HANDWRITING LARGE

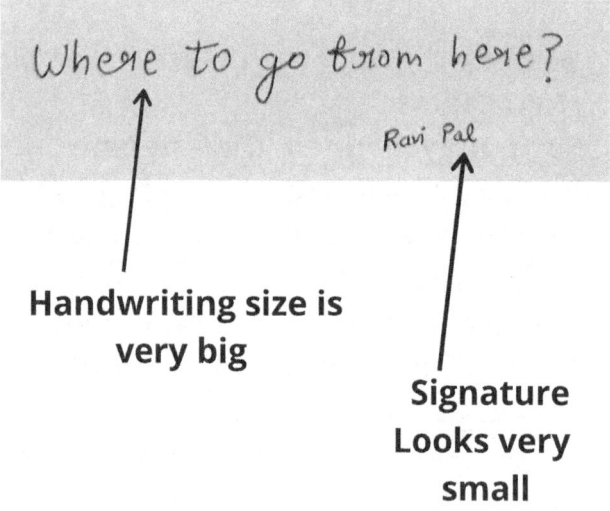

Handwriting size is very big

Signature Looks very small

HOW TO FIND?

- Signature size is very small compared to handwriting

WHAT IT INDICATES?

- These people also want attention yet they don't brag about it or even try to get it
- You may find this person standing alone in corner of a event, party or group photo.
- Our eyes are drawn to this as it is not normal
- Self-centered personality
- At home they are very interactive

WHO SIGN LIKE THIS?

Writers who indirectly get our attention by looking like a mysterious person

SIGN STRAIGHT, HANDWRITING RIGHTWARD

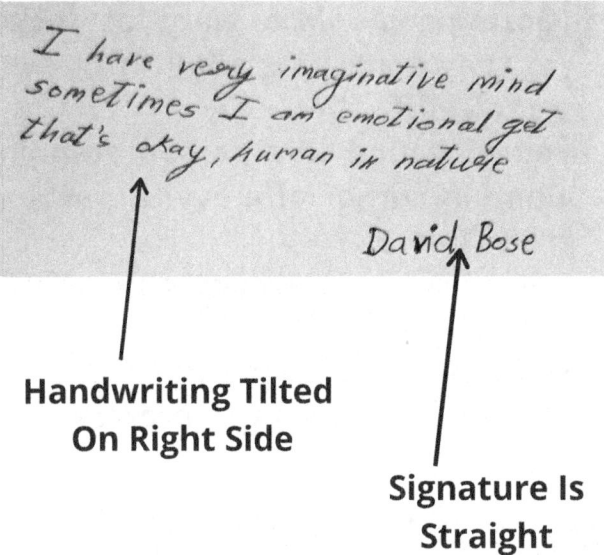

I have very imaginative mind
sometimes I am emotional get
that's okay, human in nature

David Bose

Handwriting Tilted On Right Side

Signature Is Straight

HOW TO FIND?

- Handwriting is having Right Slant while signature is having Straight Slant

WHAT IT INDICATES?

- By just looking at sample you will automatically get idea that this person is not his true self in public.
- In public they may show that they are logical person, not emotional, strong yet in reality they are opposite
- They are emotional people in reality who make decisions based on emotions.

WHO SIGN LIKE THIS?

Emotional in reality yet tries show they are logical

SIGN RIGHTWARD,
HANDWRITING STRAIGHT

Today is a good day, I am happy & grateful to universe for everything. Thank You!

Jatin Bhoir

Handwriting Is Straight

Signature Is Rightward

196] LOOK AND ANALYZE

HOW TO FIND?

- Handwriting is having Straight Slant while signature is having Right Slant

WHAT IT INDICATES?

- These writers will act like a friendly person & will show more emotions when they are in front of people in public life
- At home you will find them being cold or less emotional and more rational.
- More the rightward slant or angle in sign more the writer show emotions in public yet in private life he/she is opposite

WHO SIGN LIKE THIS?

Writers who are Emotional in public Rational at home

SIGN LEFTWARD, HANDWRITING RIGHTWARD

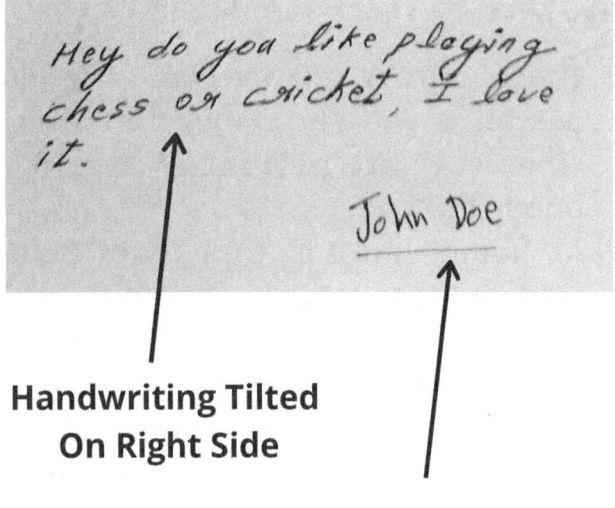

Hey do you like playing chess or cricket, I love it.

John Doe

Handwriting Tilted On Right Side

Signature Is Leftward

HOW TO FIND?

- Handwriting is having Right Slant while signature is having Left Slant

WHAT IT INDICATES?

- Rare type sample yet these writers do exist
- Leftward sign indicates that writer in public will not share his/her feelings, emotions with anyone and would most likely be in behind the scenes
- Yet at home he/she likes to be more vulnerable or emotional, creative.
- Writer may have some trust issues with strangers the reason for this behaviour.

WHO SIGN LIKE THIS?

Writers who at home are more emotional while at public place they are more rational

---

SIGN RIGHTWARD, HANDWRITING LEFT

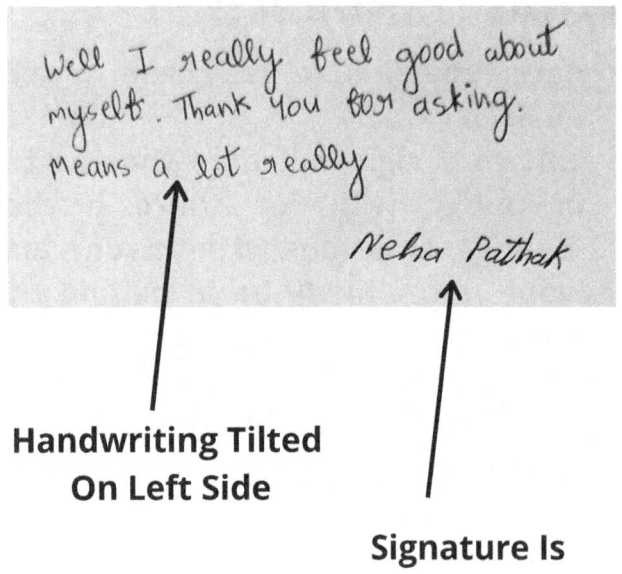

Well I really feel good about myself. Thank you for asking. Means a lot really

Neha Pathak

Handwriting Tilted On Left Side

Signature Is Rightward

200] LOOK AND ANALYZE

HOW TO FIND?

- Handwriting is having Left Slant while signature is having Right Slant

WHAT IT INDICATES?

- Writer in front of others act like a warm, outgoing person yet in reality they have reserved private personality.
- They are often secretive in nature about their private life so you need to gain their trust to know them fully

WHO SIGN LIKE THIS?

Very Rare Individuals

LEGIBLE HANDWRITING, SIGNATURE

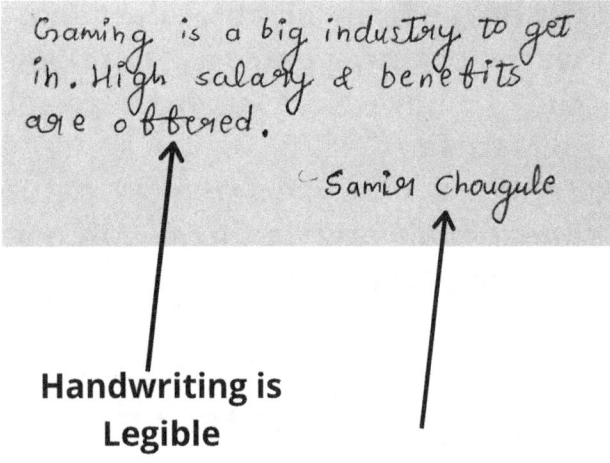

Handwriting is Legible

Signature Is Legible (Easy to read)

HOW TO FIND?

- Handwriting is Legible or readable and signature is also same

WHAT IT INDICATES?

- Firstly legibility means writer is more open minded & doesn't feel any need to hide anything.
- Writer here want to communicate about who they are.
- Here he/she is more communicative about their public as well as private persona
- You will find this trait in many samples as this is a common trait to be found

WHO SIGN LIKE THIS?

Writers who are openminded

ILLEGIBLE HANDWRITING, SIGNATURE

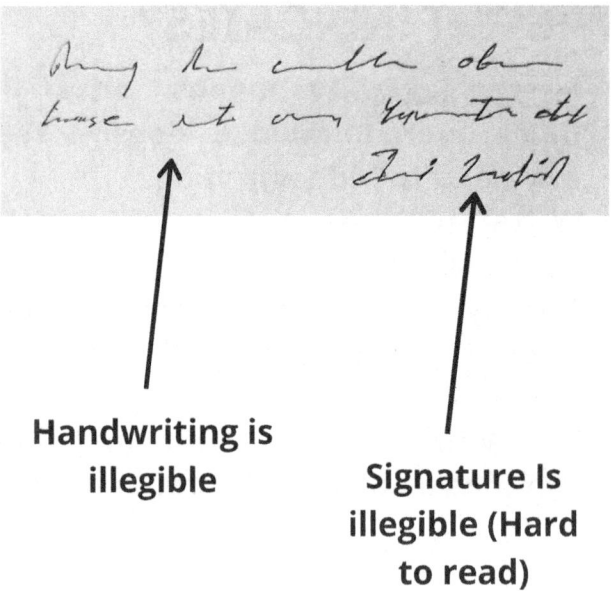

Handwriting is illegible

Signature Is illegible (Hard to read)

HOW TO FIND?

- Handwriting is illegible or not readable and signature is also same

WHAT IT INDICATES?

- They may have some form of illness or are impatient in nature who don't like to be read by others.
- On inside they are lonely, little unstable as well
- Illegibility is caused due to extreme unhappiness.
- If both handwriting, sign have this then it means writer is not communicative & is unhappy

WHO SIGN LIKE THIS?

Writers who have reserved personality

ILLEGIBLE SIGN, LEGIBLE HANDWRITING

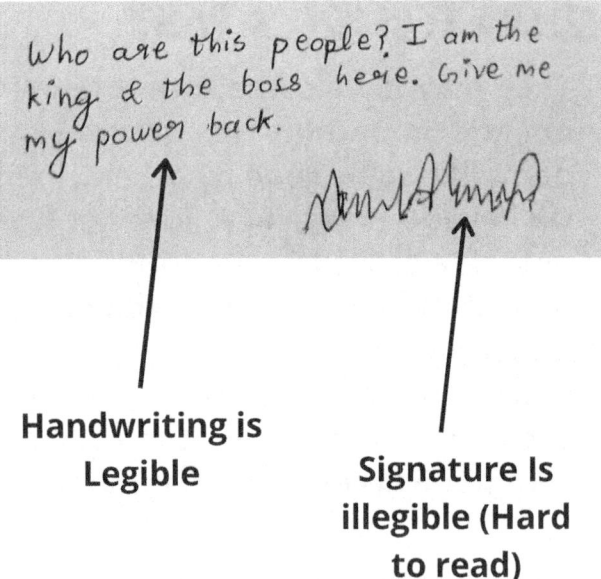

Handwriting is Legible

Signature Is illegible (Hard to read)

HOW TO FIND?

- Handwriting is legible or readable and signature is illegible

WHAT IT INDICATES?

- Secretive in nature, reserved, impatient in public yet less secretive at home or around close people
- This is also another most found type in samples
- It may also happen that writer was in hurry and henceforth signed like this.
- Do ask the writer if he/she always sign like this

WHO SIGN LIKE THIS?

Writers who are impatient in public and patient at home

LEGIBLE SIGN, ILLEGIBLE HANDWRITING

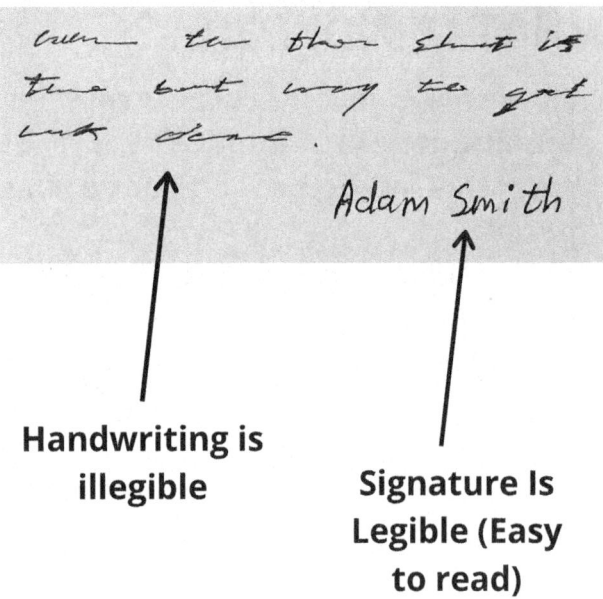

Handwriting is illegible

Signature Is Legible (Easy to read)

HOW TO FIND?

- Handwriting is illegible or not readable and signature is legible

WHAT IT INDICATES?

- Very unusual type of sample, you may find this rarely
- Writer do not want to communicate his true thoughts.
- They only care about themselves
- Caused due to mental disturbance, immaturity
- These individuals have very high ego

WHO SIGN LIKE THIS?

Writers who have high ego

SAME SIGN,
HANDWRITING

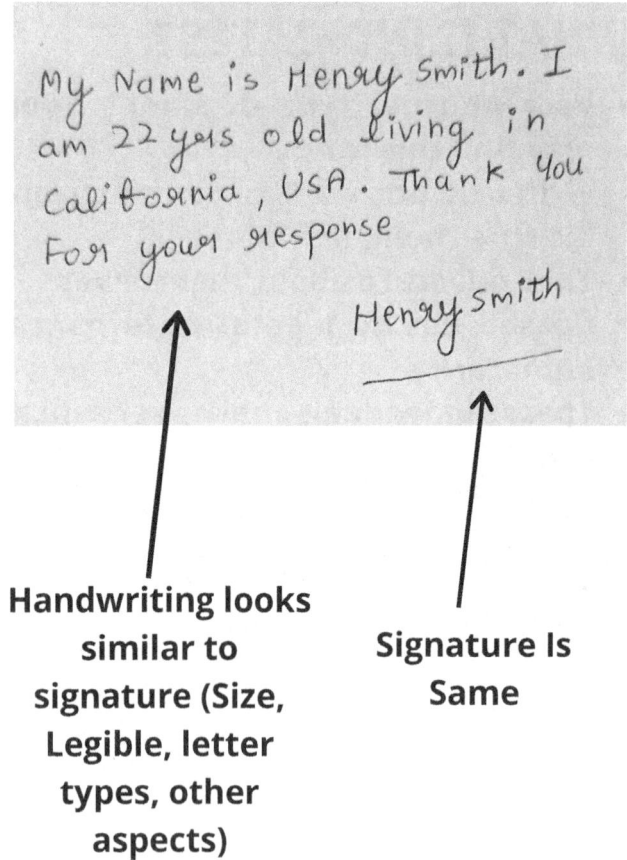

Handwriting looks similar to signature (Size, Legible, letter types, other aspects)

Signature Is Same

HOW TO FIND?

- Handwriting and Signature both have similar traits

WHAT IT INDICATES?

- Here we look at the way letters and other aspects are written in both sign, handwriting
- If a writer have most letters, other aspects same then it indicates they have same sign, handwriting.
- It indicates that writer shows their true self in public.
- Now if they are introvert in real life then in public too they will appear same, same goes for confidence levels, social life, other things

WHO SIGN LIKE THIS?

True Individuals

Analysis

TIME FOR DEMO

213] LOOK AND ANALYZE

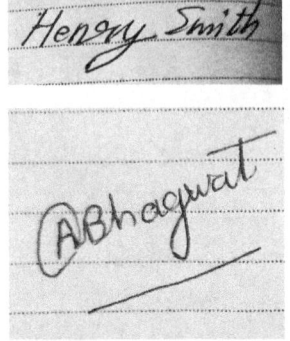

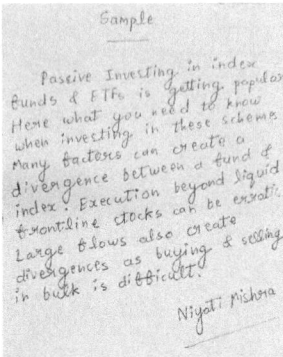

Follow below steps to do analysis, with time & experience you will be able to create your own steps, way of analysis

Step 1: Sample

1. **Tell writer to sign at least 3 times with blue/black pen on a blank or single line ruled paper**
2. **If possible take handwriting sample as well**
3. **Ask the writer what name they have written up. Eg- first name or last name or other**
4. **Sometimes a writer may have different types of sign, ask them to give all the types and let you know which one do they use the most.**

17

Analysis Steps

Step 2: Scanning & Noting

1. Which name is written? Spacing is correct or not? (If two names are present)
2. Name legible or illegible
3. How many underlines? Dots?
4. Check Direction & Slant
5. Size too
6. Is there any emotional distress or negative trait?
7. Letter traits (t, y, i, other letters)
8. Where is sign placed?
9. Check speed if writer is signing in front of you
10. Is it same as the handwriting? (Conditions)
11. What can you say about writer's public personality (summary)
12. Any suggestions for improvements?

Step 3: Explanation: The PNC Method

1. Positive Traits
2. Negative Traits
3. Improvements or Changes

215] LOOK AND ANALYZE

ANALYSIS SHORT DEMO - ONLY 1 NAME

1]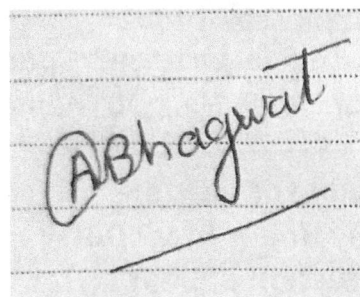

Positive Points:

1. First name initial and full last name is present which shows writer is someone who make sacrifice for others. Hardworking person
2. Upward signature shows good optimism. Writer likes to be in front as a leader.
3. Writer is someone who have personal values and follow principles to live their life. Single underline

4. Want to be seen as a confident person who dream big. High t bar is present

- **Now let's look at things which needs improvement--**

  1. Writer is having circle around "A" only not around last name which shows writer is trying to protect their emotions from outside influence
  2. Self-blame, writer blames himself even when their mistake is not there

- **Changes writer must do:**

  1. Remove the circle and write A clearly

- **In the beginning just do the analysis and don't try to suggest more than 2 changes. After gaining 1-2 year experience you can suggest more**
- **Also try to be human so instead of "Private person" you can say "Writer is a private person who doesn't just open up to new people"**
- **Mention the trait as well. For Eg- First Name shows writer is independent. (It helps in building trust that you are saying according to trait not from your imagination)**

ANALYSIS SHORT DEMO - TWO NAMES

2]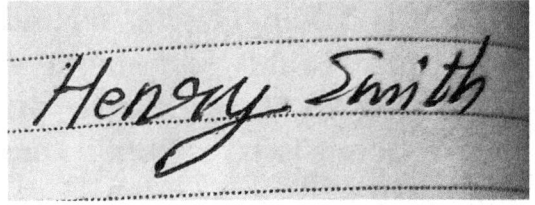

Positive Points:

1. Here both first name and last name is present which shows writer have balanced approach towards life
2. Writer gives equal priority to family as well as self or personal as well as professional goals
3. Rightward slant shows creativity, writer can work best in creative field.
4. Signature is in straight direction, writer likes working behind the scenes & is ok if not being recognized

5. Pointed m shows fast thinking & intelligence. Quick learner

- **Now let's look at things which needs improvement--**
1. **Writer is emotional in nature so if writer is facing problem because of being emotional then it needs to be changed**
2. **Spacing between first name and last name is more. Writer doesn't feel close with the family**

- **Changes writer must do:**
1. **Decrease the spacing between names**
2. **Write sign with straight slant if writer is facing issues due to being emotional**

- **Again, In the beginning just do the analysis and don't try to suggest more than 2 changes. After gaining 1-2 year experience you can suggest more (VERY IMPORTANT)**

219] LOOK AND ANALYZE

ANALYSIS SHORT DEMO - HANDWRITING + SIGN

3]

Sample

Passive Investing in index
Bunds & ETFs is getting popular
Here what you need to know
when investing in these schemes.
Many Bactors can create a
divergence between a fund &
index. Execution beyond liquid
Brontline stocks can be erratic
Large Blows also create
divergences as buying & selling
in bulk is difficult.

Niyati Mishra

Positive Points:

1. **Both handwriting and signature is going in upward direction which shows writer is truly an optimistic person who doesn't give up easily.**
2. **Signature size little larger than handwriting which shows healthy**

social confidence.

3. Balance person who gives equal importance to self, family. Both names are present

4. Organized person in nature as both handwriting and sign have dot right above i bar

5. Future oriented person as sign is placed on right side

- Now let's look at things which needs improvement--

1. Need to increase pressure to increase energy levels

- Changes writer must do:

1. Increase the pressure of handwriting as well signature

Graphotheraphy

IMPROVE SOMEONE'S SIGNATURE!

GRAPHOTHERAPHY

How Does It Work?

What if you do reverse of Graphology? Change your signature, handwriting in a particular way?

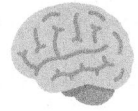

Well that will develop new cells, signals in the brain & that new feelings, emotions will then get accepted by your brain

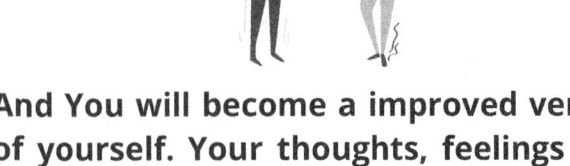

And You will become a improved version of yourself. Your thoughts, feelings gets improved

18

Graphotheraphy

- In Simple Words, Graphotheraphy is the way of improving someone's personality, career, relationships, life by changing their handwriting, signature. Just like psychotherapy
- One of the easiest method to improve your life!
- Graphology is where we look at brain's output while Graphotheraphy is where we give new inputs to the brain
- How many days to practice? It depends on person to person. Some people are able to implement changes quickly while it takes time for some people.
- Practice the trait until it becomes permanent part of your handwriting, signature.
- No need to rush it's a long term goal, take your own time. Normally it takes 21 days to form an habit.
- Make changes only in casual sign not the official one which is used for bank verification. So bank, imp docs sign remains same, only the casual one changes

225] LOOK AND ANALYZE

___

EXAMPLE: 1

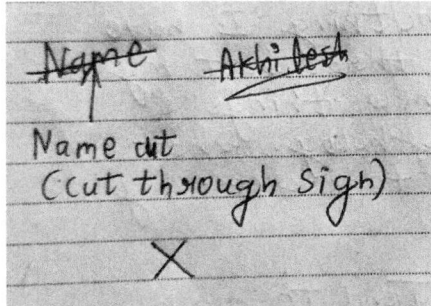

Before: Suicide sign

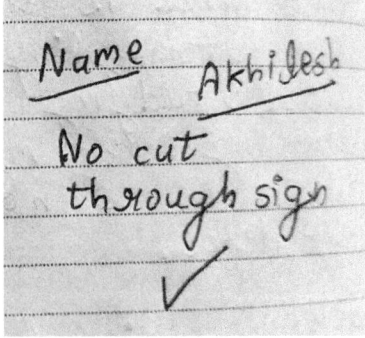

After

- **Remove the cut**
- **Let sign go in upward direction**
- **Put 1 underline below**

EXAMPLE: 2

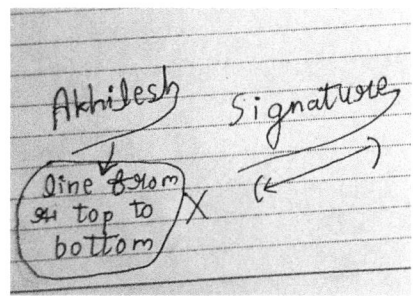

Past Thinker

Before

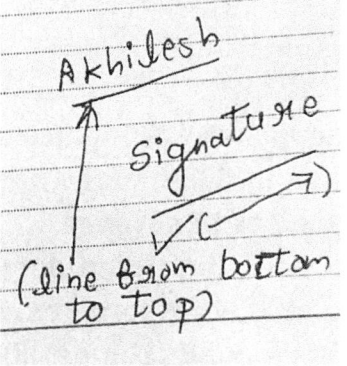

- **End last letter (no down side extend)**
- **Draw underline from bottom to top**

After

IS THERE ANY PERFECT SIGNATURE?

Good Traits

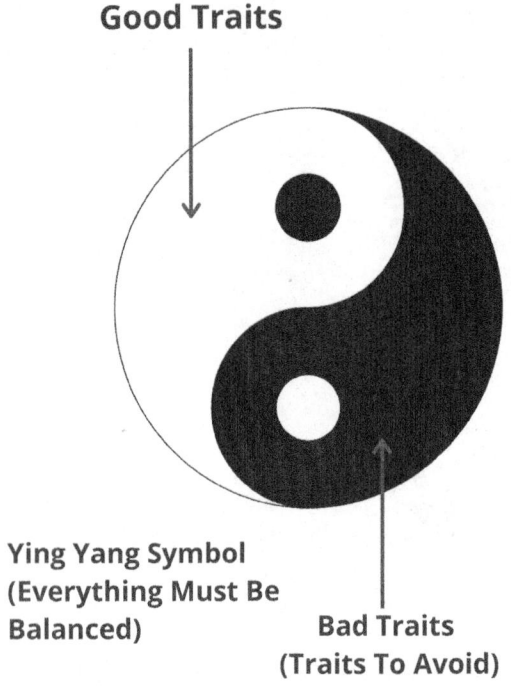

**Ying Yang Symbol
(Everything Must Be
Balanced)**

**Bad Traits
(Traits To Avoid)**

- **No this universe works on balance so almost every trait in Graphology have good things as well as bad things.**
- **High t bar indicates high confidence as well as high ego. Now some traits indeed only have bad things like suicide sign.**

NO PERFECT SIGNATURE

- Yet there is no perfect handwriting or sign, even a Graphologist doesn't have a perfect one!
- Still there are some positive traits which everyone should have.
- Top 10 Tips For An Ideal Signature!
1. First letter of First Name, Last Name or any initials must always be capital.
2. Medium Size is ideal, too large or too small is not good
3. Single Underline is best
4. First Name + Last Name is a good choice (Your Choice Matters Though)
5. Medium pressure
6. Legible sign is always good
7. Upward direction
8. Letters in sign must match your handwriting
9. On page it's best to place sign on right side
10. Keep it simple (Best Advice)

ACKNOWLEDGMENTS

- I believe no one is self-made as we only grow when we help each other. There are many people behind someone's success.
- Firstly, I would like to thank all the Graphologymadesimple (GMS) community members for their support. Without them I wouldn't have been able to come this far. The bullet point method of explanation was suggested by community members (Instagram Poll)
- Secondly, I am grateful for all the Graphologists who have been spreading this knowledge from many years. I would also like to thank all the writers, authors, bloggers, video creators, Instagram pages, other social media pages who have been spreading this valuable knowledge globally on a regular basis. Because of those people I was able to learn graphology and create this book.

231] LOOK AND ANALYZE

WHERE TO GO FROM HERE?

If you want to learn complete Graphology then Graphologymadesimple is a right place for you!

You can learn graphology handwriting + sign analysis through different ways like
1. **Posts**
2. **Blogs**
3. **Videos**
4. **Courses (Free + Paid)**
5. **Mail, Q&A**

You can also get your analysis done or Hire me as a speaker for your event!

- **Just Google "Graphologymadesimple"**

RESOURCES

- Google "Graphologymadesimple" to find all our social media links as well

.• Here's A Free Signature Analysis Online Course: <u>bit.ly/gmsfreesignaturecourse</u>

- Or Scan This QR Code To Get Your Free Sign Analysis Course:

- <u>Graphology Newsletter:</u>
<u>http://newsletters.graphologymadesimple.com/</u>

- <u>Website (Learn Complete Graphology):</u>
<u>www.graphologymadesimple.com</u>

ABOUT THE AUTHOR

Akhilesh Bhagwat

- Akhilesh Bhagwat is a Technologist & a Behavioral Scientist who is also a Graphology Expert & Founder of Graphologymadesimple & Allin1hub. He has successfully completed 500+ handwriting, signature analysis of people from 25+ different countries with 98% success rate.

- Along with analysis he has also helped people improve their personality by suggesting the right changes in handwriting as well as signature. If you are on Instagram, Facebook then you can check Graphologymadesimple page.

- Connect with me on:

- <u>My Personal Website:</u> www.iakhileshbhagwat.home.blog/

- <u>LinkedIn:</u> www.linkedin.com/in/akhileshbhagwat

- <u>Twitter:</u> www.twitter.com/bhagwatakhilesh

- Or Just <u>Google "Akhilesh Bhagwat"</u>

You Can Now Do
Signature Analysis
Of Any Random
Signature!

*Keep Learning
And
Keep Growing!*

Printed in Great Britain
by Amazon

23303728R00139